# Mrs Packlet...
## and Othe...

*In a world that is supposed to be moved by hunger and by love, ...*
*was an exception: her movements and motives were largely determined by dis-*
*like of Loona Bimberton.*

Mrs Packletide wants a better story to tell than her enemy, Loona Bimberton – so she decides to shoot a tiger. A respectable church historian takes a sudden shocking interest in a lady's female servant. A house party is ruined by a talking cat.

Just three of the twelve strange situations in this book of short stories – situations that could only come from the unusual mind of Saki, one of the greatest – and cruellest – short story writers of the century.

Saki knew upper class English society well – and he had no mercy for it. In these stories he attacks the world he grew up in. Among them are some of the funniest stories in the English language.

Saki was the pen-name of Hector Hugh Munro, who was born to British parents in Burma in 1870. At the age of two, after the death of his mother, he was sent to England with his brother and sister and brought up in Devon by two aunts. The unmarried aunts hated each other and disliked children, so he did not have a happy home life.

Munro himself never married and had a difficult adult life. He worked as a police officer in Burma for a short while, but gave it up after a serious illness. Back in Britain, he decided to earn a living by writing and began by writing mainly for newspapers. He took the name 'Saki' from a famous poem by Omar Khayyam, an Iranian poet.

From 1902 to 1908 he was foreign correspondent for the *Morning Post* in Paris, Poland and Russia. He published his first book of short stories in 1904. When the First World War began, he chose to serve as an ordinary soldier, rather than as an officer, and was killed in 1916. Little is known of his private life, as his sister destroyed all his papers after his death.

OTHER TITLES IN THE SERIES

# Mrs Packletide's Tiger

## and Other Stories

## SAKI (H. H. MUNRO)

Level 6

Retold by J. Y. K. Kerr
Series Editor: Derek Strange

PENGUIN BOOKS

PENGUIN BOOKS

Published by the Penguin Group
Penguin Books Ltd, 27 Wrights Lane, London W8 5TZ, England
Penguin Books USA Inc., 375 Hudson Street, New York, New York 10014, USA
Penguin Books Australia Ltd, Ringwood, Victoria, Australia
Penguin Books Canada Ltd, 10 Alcorn Avenue, Toronto, Ontario, Canada M4V 3B2
Penguin Books (NZ) Ltd, 182–190 Wairau Road, Auckland 10, New Zealand

Penguin Books Ltd, Registered Offices: Harmondsworth, Middlesex, England

This adaptation published by Penguin Books 1993
3 5 7 9 10 8 6 4 2

Illustrations by Chris Chaisty (David Lewis Illustrators)

Typeset by Datix International Limited, Bungay, Suffolk
Printed in England by Clays Ltd, St Ives plc
Set in 11/13 pt Lasercomp Bembo

# Mrs Packletide's Tiger and Other Stories

## *To the teacher:*

In addition to all the language forms of Levels One to Five, which are used again at this level of the series, the main verb forms and tenses used at Level Six are:

- future perfect verbs, passives with continuous or perfect aspects and the 'third' conditional with continuous forms
- modal verbs: *needn't* and *needn't have* (to express absence of necessity), *would* (to describe habitual past actions), *should* and *should have* (to express probability or failed expectation), *may have* and *might have* (to express possibility), *could have* and *would have* (to express past, unfulfilled possibility or likelihood).

Also used are:

- non-defining relative clauses.

Specific attention is paid to vocabulary development in the Vocabulary Work exercises at the end of the book. These exercises are aimed at training students to enlarge their vocabulary systematically through intelligent reading and effective use of a dictionary.


## *To the student:*

Dictionary Words:

- As you read this book, you will find that some words are in darker black ink than the others on the page. Look them up in your dictionary, if you do not already know them, or try to guess the meaning of the words first, and then look them up later, to check.

# Fate and Martin Stoner

In the fading light of a dull autumn afternoon, Martin Stoner made his way heavily along muddy country roads and uneven tracks that led he knew not where. Somewhere in front of him, he believed, lay the sea, and towards the sea his footsteps seemed determined to take him. Why he was struggling on to that goal he could scarcely have explained. Like a wounded animal pursued by hunting dogs, he felt by instinct that his only way of escape was to leap into the sea. In his particular case Fate was certainly pressing him hard: hunger, tiredness and complete hopelessness had driven all other thoughts from his head, and he could hardly find the energy to wonder what force was driving him on.

Stoner was one of those unfortunate men who seem to have tried everything; his natural laziness and inability to make plans had always managed to destroy any chance of even modest success in life. Now he was desperate, and there was nothing left to try. Desperation had not stirred up any hidden reserve of energy. It was quite the opposite: this crisis in his fortunes seemed to dull his brain. With the clothes he stood up in, a halfpenny in his pocket and without a single friend or known face to turn to, with no hope either of a bed for the night or a meal the next day, Martin Stoner walked blindly forward, between damp hedges and trees wet with rain, his mind blank except for the fact that somewhere in front of him lay the sea. He was also aware that he was miserably hungry.

Soon he came to a stop by an open gateway that led into a large and rather neglected garden; there was little sign of life in it, and the farmhouse at the far end of the garden looked cold and unwelcoming. A thin rain, however, was beginning to fall, and Stoner thought that here perhaps he might find a few minutes' shelter and buy a glass of milk with his last remaining coin. Exhausted, he turned into the garden and followed a narrow stone path up to a side-door. Before he had time to knock, the door opened and a bent old man with a heavily lined face was standing there to one side of the doorway as though to let him pass in.

'Could I come in out of the rain?' Stoner began, but the old man interrupted him.

'Come in, Master Tom. I knew you would come back one of these days.'

Stoner almost fell as he stepped inside, and stood looking in disbelief at the old man.

'Sit down while I fetch you a bit of supper,' said the old man, his voice trembling in his eagerness.

Stoner's legs finally gave way and he sank into the armchair that had been pushed towards him. In another minute he was hungrily eating the cold meat, cheese and bread that had been placed on the table at his side.

'You've hardly changed these past four years,' went on the old man in a voice that sounded to Stoner like something in a dream, far away and quite unreal. 'But you'll find us greatly changed, you will. There's no one on the farm who was here when you left, just me and your old aunt. I'll go and tell her that you've come. She won't agree to see you, but she'll certainly let you stay. She always did say that if you came back you should stay, but she'd never set eyes on you or speak to you again.'

The old man placed a large glass of beer on the table in front of Stoner and then moved away slowly and painfully down a long passage. The weak rainfall had changed to heavy drops, which now beat violently against door and windows. The wanderer thought fearfully of what the seashore must look like with night falling and such heavy rain beating down. He finished the food and the beer and sat helplessly waiting for the return of his strange host. As the grandfather clock in the corner counted the minutes, a new hope began to grow in the young man's mind; his former urgent desire for food and a few minutes' rest now became the need to find a night's shelter under this seemingly friendly roof. The sound of footsteps in the passage announced the old farm servant's return.

'The old lady won't see you, Master Tom, but she says you are to stay. And that's only right, seeing that the farm will be yours when she's dead and gone. I've had a fire lit in your room, Master Tom, and the girls have put fresh sheets on the bed. You'll find nothing has changed up there. Maybe you're tired and would like to go there now?'

Without a word, Martin Stoner rose heavily to his feet and followed the kindly old man along a passage, up a short wooden staircase, along another passage and into a large room lit with a fire burning cheerfully. There was not much furniture; what there was in the room was plain, old-fashioned and good of its kind. A furry animal in a glass case and a wall calendar of four years ago were about the only forms of decoration. But Stoner had eyes for little else than the bed and could hardly wait to tear the clothes off himself before rolling in the luxury of its comfortable depths. Merciless Fate seemed to have stopped pursuing him, at least for the moment.

In the cold light of morning Stoner laughed without joy as he slowly realized the position in which he now found himself. Perhaps he might hurriedly eat a bit of breakfast on the strength of his likeness to this other missing trouble-maker, and get safely away before anyone discovered the deception which had been so easy to carry out. In the room downstairs he found the bent old man ready with a dish of bacon and fried eggs for 'Master Tom's' breakfast, while a hard-faced woman poured him a cup of tea. As he sat at the table, a small dog came up and wanted to make friends with him.

'That's old Bowker's son,' explained the old man, whom the hard-faced woman servant called by the name of George. 'She was always fond of you; it never seemed the same after you went away to Australia. She died about a year ago. It's her son.'

Stoner found it difficult to regret this death: old Bowker would have been quick to recognize that he was not her master.

'You'll go for a ride, Master Tom?' was the next unexpected suggestion that came from the old man. 'We have a nice little brown horse that's a pleasure to ride. Old Biddy is getting on in years, though she goes well still, but I'll have the little brown one made ready and brought round to the door.'

'I've got no riding things,' said Martin, almost laughing as he looked down at his only suit of well-worn clothes.

'Master Tom,' said the old man earnestly, almost offended it seemed, 'all your things are just as you left them. We'll put them to air in front of the fire and they'll be all right. It will take your mind off things to do a bit of riding and shooting now and again. You'll find the people round here have hard and bitter attitudes towards you. They haven't forgotten or forgiven. No one will come near you, so you'd best get what pleasure you can with the horse and the dog. They're good company, too.'

Old George hurried away to give his orders, and Stoner, feeling more than ever like someone in a dream, went upstairs to inspect 'Master Tom's' riding clothes. A ride was one of the pleasures dearest to his heart, and the fact that none of Tom's former companions were likely to come near him offered some protection against the possible discovery of who he really was. As he put on Tom's riding clothes, which fitted reasonably well, he wondered idly what kind of crime the real Tom had committed to set the whole neighbourhood against him. The sound of the horse being brought round to the side-door cut these reflections short.

'I'm a beggar on horseback,' thought Stoner to himself, as he rode rapidly along the muddy roads where he had yesterday walked as a tramp. And then dismissing even this idea, he gave himself up to the pleasure of riding at full speed along the grassy edge of a level half-mile of road. At an open gateway he paused to allow two carts to turn into a field. The young men driving the carts looked at him long and hard and, as he passed by, he heard an excited voice call out: 'It's Tom Prike! I knew him at once; so he's showing himself here again, is he?'

Clearly the likeness which had deceived an old man standing close beside him was good enough to mislead younger eyes at a short distance.

During his ride he met with plenty of evidence that local people had neither forgotten nor forgiven the past crime which he had taken over from the absent Tom. Dark looks and unfriendly comments greeted him when-ever he met human beings. 'Bowker's son' running by his side seemed the one friendly creature in an unfriendly world.

As he got down from the horse at the side-door, he caught sight for a moment of a thin, elderly woman watching him from behind the curtain of an upper window. He was fairly sure that this was his aunt by adoption.

Over the large and satisfying midday meal that was waiting for him, Stoner was able to consider the possibilities of his extraordinary situation. The real Tom, after four years of absence, might suddenly appear at the farm, or a letter might come from him at any moment. Or else, as the person to whom the farm would one day belong, the false Tom might be asked to sign documents, which could put him in an embarrassing position. Or a relation might arrive who would not choose to keep apart from him as the aunt had decided to do. All of these things would lead to his being found out. On the other hand, the other choice before him was the open sky and the muddy paths that led down to the sea. The farm at least offered a temporary shelter from poverty. Farming was one of the many things he had 'tried' in the past, and he would be able to do a certain amount of work in exchange for the kindness which he so little deserved.

'Will you have cold pork for your supper?' asked the hard-faced woman as she cleared the table. 'Or will you have it heated up?'

'Hot, with vegetables,' said Stoner. It was the only time in his life that he had made a rapid decision. And, as he gave the order, he knew that he meant to stay.

Stoner used only those parts of the house which seemed to be available to him. When he took part in the farm work, he worked as a person under orders rather than one who gave them. Old George, the brown horse and the friendly dog were his only companions in a world that was otherwise cold, silent and full of enemies. Of the owner of the farm – the old lady – he saw nothing. Once, when he knew that she had gone to church, he made a secret visit to the sitting-room in an attempt to gather some sort of knowledge of the young man whose place he had taken and whose bad reputation had become attached to himself. There were many family photographs hanging on the walls or displayed on side-tables; but the face he was searching for was not among them. At last, in a book pushed into a corner out of sight, he came across what he wanted. There was a whole series of pictures labelled

'Tom': a fat child of three in a girlish dress, an awkward-looking boy of about twelve holding a football as if he hated it, a rather good-looking youth of eighteen with very smooth, carefully parted hair, and finally a young man with a rather dissatisfied, challenging expression. Stoner examined this last photograph with particular interest: the likeness to himself was unmistakable.

From Old George, who was talkative enough on most subjects, he tried again and again to learn something of the nature of the misdeed which had caused him to be hated and avoided by his fellow men.

'What do the people around here say about me?' he asked one day, as they were walking home from a distant field.

The old man shook his head. 'They feel bitter against you, bitter indeed. Ay, it's a sad business, a sad business.'

And he was never able to persuade George to say anything more informative.

On a clear frosty morning a few days before Christmas, Stoner stood in a corner of the garden from where there was a wide view of the surrounding countryside. Here and there he cold see points of light from lamps and candles, which told of human homes where domestic happiness and the celebrations of the season had already begun. Behind him lay the dark, silent farmhouse where no one ever laughed, where even a quarrel would have seemed a welcome change. As he turned to look at the long grey front of the building, a door opened and George hurried out. Stoner heard his adopted name being called in a voice full of anxiety. Immediately he knew that something serious must have happened. His mood changed at once: the farmhouse once more seemed to him a place of peace and contentment, from which he felt unwilling to be driven.

'Master Tom,' said the old man in a throaty whisper, 'you must slip away quietly from here for a few days.

Michael Ley is back in the village, and he swears he'll shoot you if he comes across you. He'll do it, too, I can see murder in his eye. Get away under cover of night. It's only for a week or so, as he won't be here longer.'

'But where am I to go?' said Stoner, suddenly unsure of himself, because the old man's obvious terror had infected him.

'Go right away along the coast to Punchford and keep yourself hidden there. When Michael's safely gone, I'll ride the brown horse over to the Green Dragon Inn at Punchford. When you see the horse outside the Green Dragon, it's a sign that you can come back again.'

'But . . .' began Stoner hesitatingly.

'You'll be all right for money,' said the old man. 'The old lady agrees you'd best do as I say, and she's given me this.' The old man produced three gold coins and some odd pieces of silver.

Stoner felt more than ever that he was cheating these good people as he crept away that night through the back gate of the farm, with the old woman's money in his pocket. Old George and the young dog stood watching him in silence from the door of the house. He could not believe that he would ever come back, and he felt a sudden pain of regret for those two humble friends who would go on waiting earnestly for his return. Some day perhaps the real Tom would come back and there would be wild amazement among those simple people on the farm as to the real identity of the shadowy guest whom they had sheltered under their roof.

He felt no immediate anxiety about his own fate. Three pounds does not go far in the world if there's nothing behind it, but to a man who has counted his wealth in pennies it seems a good starting-point. Fortune had done him a surprisingly kind turn: when he had last stepped along these paths, he had been a hopeless adventurer, but now there might be the chance of his finding some work and making a fresh start.

As he got further from the farm, his optimistic mood grew. There was a sense of relief in becoming once more his real self and no longer feeling like the uneasy ghost of someone else. He hardly bothered to consider Michael Ley, the merciless enemy who had appeared from nowhere into his life. Since that life was now behind him, one more unreal item made very little difference. For the first time in many months he began to whistle softly to himself a carefree, happy tune.

Then, from the shadow of a huge tree a man with a gun stepped out. There was no need to wonder who he might be: the moonlight falling on his hard white face showed an expression of human hate that Stoner in all the ups and downs of his wandering life had never seen before. He leapt aside in a desperate attempt to break through the hedge that lined the pathway, but the tough branches held him back. Merciless Fate had waited for him patiently on those narrow roads, and this time Fate was not to be denied.

## Fur

'You look worried, dear,' said Eleanor.

'I *am* worried,' admitted Suzanne. 'You see, it's my birthday next week —'

'You lucky person!' interrupted Eleanor. 'My birthday doesn't come till the end of March.'

'Well, old Bertram Kneyght is over in England just now from Argentina. He's a kind of distant cousin of my mother's and so enormously rich that we've never let the relationship drop out of sight. Even if we don't see him for years, he is always Cousin Bertram when he does appear. I can't say he's ever been of much real use to us, but yesterday the subject of my birthday was mentioned and he asked me to let him know what I wanted for a present.'

'*Now* I understand the anxiety,' remarked Eleanor.

'Usually when one is faced with a problem like that,' said Suzanne, 'all one's ideas fly from one's head, one doesn't seem to have a desire in the world. Now it so happens that I've become very fond of a little Dresden figure that I saw somewhere in Kensington; about three pounds something – much more than I can afford. I very nearly gave Bertram the address of the shop; and then I suddenly thought that three pounds something was a totally inadequate sum for a man of his huge wealth to spend on a birthday present. He could spend thirty something pounds as easily as you or I could buy a bunch of violets. I don't want to be greedy, of course, but I don't like being wasteful.'

'The question is,' said Eleanor, 'what are his ideas about present-giving? Some of the wealthiest people have strangely narrow views on that subject. When people grow rich gradually, their needs and standard of living increase too, while their present-giving instincts often remain in the undeveloped condition of their earlier days. Something showy and not too expensive in a shop is their only idea of the perfect gift. That's why even quite good shops have their windows and counters crowded with things labelled "seasonable gifts", which look more expensive than they cost but which cost far more than they're worth.'

'I know,' said Suzanne. 'That's why it's so risky not to be absolutely clear when one is giving indications of one's wants. Now if I say to him: "I'm going out to Davos this winter, so anything to do with travel would be acceptable", he *might* give me a dressing-case with gold handles; but, on the other hand, he might give me a guidebook on Switzerland or *Skiing without Tears* or something of that sort.'

'He would be more likely to say: "She'll be going to Switzerland in the winter, so an umbrella is sure to be useful."'

'Yes, and I've got plenty of umbrellas, so you see where the danger and anxiety lie. Now if there's one thing more than another that I really urgently want, it's furs. I simply haven't got any. I'm told that Davos is full of Russians, and they are sure to be wearing the most lovely things. To be among people who are covered with furs when one hasn't any oneself makes one want to break most of the Ten Commandments.'\*

'If it's furs you want,' said Eleanor, 'you'll have to direct the choice of them in person. You can't be sure your cousin knows the difference between silver **fox** and rabbit.'

'There are some heavenly silver-fox wraps at Goliath and Mastodon's,' said Suzanne with a sigh. 'If I could only persuade Bertram to step into their building, and take him for a little walk through the fur department!'

'He lives somewhere near here, doesn't he?' said Eleanor. 'Do you know what his habits are? Does he take a walk at any particular time of day?'

'He usually walks down to his club about three o'clock, if it's a fine day. That takes him right past Goliath and Mastodon's.'

'Let us two meet him accidentally at the street corner tomorrow,' said Eleanor. 'We can walk a little way with him, and with luck we ought to be able to guide him into the shop. You can say you want to get a hair net or something. When we're safely there, I can say: "I wish

---

\* The Ten Commandments are ten religious rules which Christians and Jews are expected to observe.

you'd tell me what you want for your birthday." Then you'll have everything ready to hand – the rich cousin, the fur department and the topic of birthday presents.'

'It's a great idea,' said Suzanne. 'You really are an enormous support to me. Come round tomorrow at twenty to three. Don't be late, we must carry out our attack to the minute.'

At a few minutes to three the next afternoon, the fur-trappers walked cautiously towards the selected corner. In the near distance rose the enormous mass of Messrs Goliath and Mastodon's famous department store. The afternoon was brilliantly fine, exactly the sort of weather to tempt a gentleman of advancing years to take a gentle walk.

'I say, dear, I wish you'd do something for me this evening,' said Eleanor to her companion, as they waited. 'Just drop in after dinner, giving some excuse or other, and stay on to make a fourth player at cards with Adela and the aunts. Otherwise I shall have to play, and Harry Scarisbrooke is going to come in unexpectedly at about nine-fifteen. I particularly wanted to be free to talk with him while the others are playing.'

'Sorry, my dear, no can do,' said Suzanne. 'All card games with such painfully slow players as your aunts are so boring that I nearly fall asleep over them.'

'But I most particularly want an opportunity to talk with Harry,' urged Eleanor, an angry light coming into her eye.

'Sorry, I'll do anything for you, but not that,' said Suzanne sweetly. The sacrifices of friendship were beautiful in her eyes as long as she was not asked to make them.

Eleanor said nothing further on the subject, but the corners of her mouth rearranged themselves.

'There's our man!' exclaimed Suzanne suddenly. 'Hurry!'

Mr Bertram Kneyght greeted his cousin and her friend

with sincere warmth, and happily accepted their invitation to explore the crowded store that stood temptingly at their elbow. The plate-glass doors opened at their touch and the three of them plunged bravely into the struggling mass of buyers and onlookers.

'Is it always as full as this?' Bertram asked Eleanor.

'More or less, and the autumn sales are on just now,' she replied.

Suzanne, in her anxiety to pilot her wealthy cousin to the desired harbour of the fur department, was usually a few steps ahead of the others, coming back to them now and then if they paused for a moment at some attractive counter, with the nervous anxiety of a parent bird encouraging its young ones on their first flying expedition.

'It's Suzanne's birthday on Wednesday next,' confided Eleanor to Bertram Kneyght at a moment when Suzanne had left them unusually far behind. 'My birthday comes the day before, so we are both on the look-out for something to give each other.'

'Ah', said Bertram. 'Now perhaps you can advise me on that point. I want to give Suzanne something and I haven't the least idea what she wants.'

'She's rather a problem,' said Eleanor. 'She seems to have everything one can think of, lucky girl. An umbrella is always useful; she'll be going to Switzerland this winter. Yes, I should think an umbrella would please her more than anything. After our birthdays are over, we inspect each other's presents and I always feel terribly humble. She gets such nice things and I never have anything worth showing. You see, none of my relations or any of the people who give me presents is at all rich, so I can't expect them to do anything more than just mark the day with some modest little reminder. Two years ago an uncle on my mother's side of the family, who had been left a small amount of money, promised me a silver-fox fur for my birthday. I can't tell you how excited I was about it, how I saw myself showing it off to all my friends and enemies. Then, just at that moment, his wife died, and of course, poor man, he could not be expected to think of birthday presents at such a time. He's lived abroad ever since, and I never got my fur. Do you know, to this day I can scarcely look at a silver-fox skin in a shop window or round someone's neck without feeling ready to burst into tears. I suppose if I hadn't had the hope of getting one, I wouldn't feel that way. Look, there's the umbrella counter. Get her as nice a one as you can see – she's such a dear, dear girl.'

'Hullo, I thought I'd lost you,' said Suzanne, making her way through a bunch of shoppers who were blocking the way. 'Where's Bertram?'

'I got separated from him long ago. I thought he was on ahead with you,' said Eleanor. 'We shall never find him in this crush.'

Which turned out to be perfectly true.

'All our careful planning and plotting wasted,' said Suzanne bad-temperedly, when they had pushed their way without success through half a dozen departments. 'I can't think why you didn't keep hold of his arm,' she said to Eleanor.

'I would have done if I'd known him longer, but I'd only just been introduced. It's nearly four now, we'd better have tea.'

Some days later, Suzanne rang Eleanor up on the telephone.

'Thank you very much for the bath salts. They were just what I wanted. Very good of you. I say, do you know what that Kneyght person has given me? Just what you said he would – a miserable little umbrella! What? Oh, yes, quite a good enough umbrella in its way, but still . . .'

'You must come and see what he's given me,' came Eleanor's voice over the phone.

14

'Look, there's the umbrella counter. Get her as nice a one as you can see – she's such a dear, dear girl.'

'You! Why should he give you anything?'

'Your cousin appears to be one of those rare people of wealth who take a pleasure in giving good presents,' came the reply.

'I wondered why he was so anxious to know where she lived,' said Suzanne sharply to herself as she rang off.

A cloud has arisen over the friendship between the two young women. As far as Eleanor is concerned, the cloud has a silver-fox **lining.**★

# The Open Window

'My aunt will be down quite soon, Mr Nuttel,' said a very self-confident young lady of fifteen. 'In the meantime you must try to put up with me.'

Framton Nuttel attempted to say the correct something which would please the niece of the moment without neglecting the aunt that was to come. Privately he doubted more than ever whether these formal visits to the homes of total strangers would do much to help the cure for his nerves which he was supposed to be following.

'I know how it will be,' his sister had said, when he was preparing to set off for this distant part of the country. 'You will bury yourself down there and not speak to a living soul, and your nerves will be worse than ever because of your depression. I shall just give you letters of introduction to all the people I know there. Some of them, as far as I can remember, were quite nice.'

Framton wondered whether Mrs Sappleton, the lady to

★ The traditional saying in English is: 'Every cloud has a silver lining', meaning that even misfortunes have something good in them.

whom he was presenting one of these letters of introduction, came into the 'nice' category.

'Do you know many of the people round here?' asked the niece, when she judged that they had sat long enough in sympathetic silence.

'Hardly a soul,' said Framton. 'My sister was staying at the home of the village doctor about four years ago, and she gave me letters of introduction to some of the people here.' He made this last statement with a distinct sigh of regret.

'Then you know practically nothing about my aunt?' the confident young lady went on.

'Only her name and address,' admitted the visitor. He was wondering whether Mrs Sappleton was married or in the widowed state. There was something undefinable about the room which suggested a **masculine** presence.

'Her great tragedy happened just three years ago,' said the child. 'That would be since the time of your sister's visit.'

'Her tragedy?' asked Framton. Somehow in this restful part of the country tragedies seemed out of place.

'You may wonder why we keep that window wide open on an October afternoon,' said the niece, pointing to a large french window that opened on to a grassy area of the garden.

'It is quite warm for the time of year,' said Framton, 'but has that window got anything to do with the tragedy?'

'Out through that window, three years ago to the day, her husband and her two young brothers went off for a day's duck-shooting. They never came back. In crossing the fields to their favourite hunting-ground, they were all swallowed up in a dangerous piece of **bog**. It was that terribly wet summer, you know, and places that were safe in other years gave way suddenly, without warning. Their bodies were never found. That was the most horrible part of it.' Here the child's voice lost its usual self-control and trembled with human emotion. 'Poor aunt always thinks that they'll come back some day, they and the little brown hunting-dog that was lost with them, and that they'll walk in through that window, just as they used to do. That's why the window is kept open every evening until it's nearly dark. Poor, dear aunt, she has often told me how they went out, her husband with his white raincoat over his arm, and Ronnie, her youngest brother, singing "Bertie goes to battle", as he always did just to annoy her, because she said it got on her nerves. Do you know, sometimes on still, quiet evenings like this, I almost have the strange feeling that they will all walk through that window once again and –'

She broke off, her voice shaking. It was a relief to Framton when the aunt hurried into the room with many apologies for being late in making her appearance.

'I hope Vera has been amusing you?' she said.

'She has been very interesting,' said Framton.

'I hope you don't mind the open window,' said Mrs Sappleton brightly. 'My husband and brothers will be home soon from their shooting, and they always come this way. They've been out on the bogs today, so all that mud will make a fine mess of my poor carpets. Just like you men, isn't it?'

She chatted on happily about the shooting and the scarcity of birds and her hopes that the wild duck would return in the winter. To Framton it was all completely horrible. He made a desperate but not wholly successful effort to turn the conversation to a less frightening subject. He was conscious that his hostess was giving him only part of her attention and that her eyes were continually wandering past him to the open window and the grass beyond. It was certainly unfortunate that he had chosen to pay his visit on the very same date that this tragic event had happened.

'The doctors agree that I should have complete rest, an absence of mental excitement, and that I should avoid any kind of violent physical exercise,' announced Framton, who mistakenly believed that complete strangers are eager to know every detail about one's illnesses and disabilities, together with their causes and cures. 'On the matter of diet they are not so much in agreement,' he continued.

'Indeed?' said Mrs Sappleton in a voice which only replaced a yawn at the last moment. Then she suddenly brightened and paid close attention – but not to what Framton was saying.

'Here they are at last!' she cried. 'Just in time for tea, and just look at them – muddy up to the eyes!'

Framton's body shook slightly and he turned towards the niece with a glance meant to suggest sympathy and understanding. The child was looking hard through the open window with disbelieving horror in her eyes. With a cold shock of fear, Framton turned round in his seat and looked in the same direction.

In the deepening half-light, three figures were walking towards the window; they all carried guns and one of them wore a white raincoat hung round his shoulders. A tired brown hunting-dog kept close at their heels. Noiselessly they approached the house, and then a young, not very musical voice started singing 'Bertie goes to battle'.

Framton seized his stick and hat; the hall door, the driveway to the house and the front gate were scarcely stages in his rapid escape. A cyclist coming along the road had to run into the hedge to avoid crashing into him.

'Here we are, my dear,' said the owner of the white raincoat, coming in through the window. 'Fairly muddy, but we aren't as wet as usual. Who was that man who rushed away just as we got here?'

'A most extraordinary man, a Mr Nuttel,' said Mrs

'Here they are at last!' she cried. 'Just in time for tea, and just
look at them – muddy up to the eyes!'

Sappleton. 'He could only talk about his illnesses, and ran off without a word of goodbye or apology when you arrived. One would think that he had seen a ghost.'

'I expect it was the dog,' said the niece calmly. 'He told me he had a horror of dogs. He was once chased into a burial ground on the banks of the Ganges by a crowd of half-wild dogs and had to spend the night in a newly dug grave, with the creatures barking and grinning and baring their teeth just above him. It's enough to make anyone lose their nerve.'

She was a girl with a well-developed romantic imagination.

## The Secret Life of Septimus Brope

'Who and what is Mr Brope?' demanded Mrs Troyle, Clovis's aunt, suddenly.

Mrs Riversedge, who had been cutting off the dead heads of her roses and thinking of nothing in particular, began hurriedly to pay attention. She was one of those old-fashioned hostesses who consider that one ought to know something about one's guests, and that the something ought to be in their favour.

'I believe he comes from Leighton Buzzard,' she remarked, as a form of explanation.

'In these days of rapid and convenient travel,' said Clovis, who was destroying a large family of greenfly on a rose-**bush** with clouds of cigarette smoke, 'to come from Leighton Buzzard does not necessarily indicate any great strength of character. It might only mean restlessness. Now if he had left it because of his bad behaviour or as a protest against the foolishness of its inhabitants, that would tell us something about the man and his purpose in life.'

'What does he do?' Mrs Troyle went on severely.

'He is the editor of *Cathedral Monthly*,' said her hostess, 'and he's enormously well-informed about church architecture and furniture and the influence of the Byzantine tradition on the modern church service and all those kinds of things. Perhaps he is just a little bit heavy and buried in one range of subjects; but it takes all sorts to make a good house party, you know. You don't find him *too* dull, do you?'

'Dullness I could excuse,' said Clovis's aunt. 'What I cannot forgive is his making love to my **maid**.'

'My dear Mrs Troyle,' said her hostess in astonishment, 'what an extraordinary idea! I can promise you that Mr Brope would not dream of doing such a thing.'

'His dreams are of no importance to me; for all I care, his sleep may be full of imagined love-affairs with the entire domestic staff. But in his waking hours he shall not make love to my maid. It's no use arguing about it, I'm firm on that point.'

'But you must be mistaken,' insisted Mrs Riversedge. 'Mr Brope would be the last person to do such a thing.'

'He is the first person to do such a thing, as far as my information goes, and, if I have any say in the matter, he shall certainly be the last. Of course I am not referring to lovers with respectable intentions.'

'I simply cannot think that a man who writes so charmingly and informatively about religious buildings and Byzantine influences would behave in such an unprincipled manner,' said Mrs Riversedge. 'What evidence have you got that he's doing anything of the sort? I don't want to doubt your word, of course, but we mustn't be too ready to judge him without hearing his side of the story, must we?'

'Whether we prejudge him or not, he has certainly not been unheard. He has the room next to my dressing-room, and, on two occasions when I dare say he thought I was absent, I have plainly heard him announcing through the wall, "I love you, Florrie." The bedroom walls are very thin: one can almost hear the sound of a watch in the next room.'

'Is your maid called Florence?'

'Her name is Florinda.'

'What an extraordinary name to give a maid!'

'I did not give it to her: she already had it when she entered my service.'

'What I mean is,' said Mrs Riversedge, 'that when I get maids with unsuitable names, I call them Jane. They soon get used to it.'

'An excellent plan,' said the aunt of Clovis coldly. 'Unfortunately, I have got used to being called Jane myself. It happens to be my name.' She cut short Mrs Riversedge's flood of apologies by drily remarking: 'The question is not whether I'm to call my maid Florinda, but whether Mr Brope is to be allowed to call her Florrie. I am strongly of the opinion that he should not.'

'He may have been repeating the words of some song,' said Mrs Riversedge hopefully. 'There are lots of silly songs with girls' names in them,' she continued, turning to Clovis as a possible authority on the subject. '"You mustn't call me Mary —"'

'I shouldn't think of doing so,' Clovis said firmly. 'In the first place, I've always understood that your name was Henrietta; and then I hardly know you well enough for such familiarity.'

'I mean there's a song with those words,' Mrs Riversedge hurriedly explained, 'and there's "Carmen loves a barman" and "My girl is Pearl" and dozens of others. Certainly it doesn't sound like Mr Brope to be singing such songs, but I think we ought to give him the benefit of the doubt.'

'I had already done so,' said Mrs Troyle, 'until further evidence came my way.'

She shut her lips with the firm finality of someone enjoying the delightful certainty of being begged to open them again.

'Further evidence?' exclaimed her hostess. 'Do tell me!'

'As I was coming upstairs after breakfast, Mr Brope was just passing my room. In the most natural way in the world, a piece of paper dropped out of a packet that he held in his hand and fell to the ground just at my door. I was going to call out to him, "You've dropped something", and then for some reason I held back and didn't show myself till he was safely in his room. You see, I suddenly realized that I was very seldom in my room just at that time. So I picked up that innocent-looking piece of paper.' Mrs Troyle paused again, with the self-satisfied air of a detective who has discovered a poisonous snake in a box of chocolates.

Mrs Riversedge applied her scissors to the nearest rose-bush, accidentally cutting off a beautiful rose that was just coming into flower. 'What was on the paper?' she asked.

'Just the words in pencil, "I love you, Florrie", and then underneath, crossed out with a faint line but perfectly plain to read, "Meet me in the garden by the **lilac** tree."'

'There *is* a lilac tree at the bottom of the garden,' admitted Mrs Riversedge.

'At any rate he appears to be truthful,' commented Clovis.

'To think that a **scandal** of this sort should be going on under my roof!' said Mrs Riversedge, greatly annoyed.

'I wonder why it is that scandal seems so much worse under a roof,' remarked Clovis. 'I've always considered it as evidence of the superiority of cats that they perform most of their scandals on top of the roof, not under it.'

'Now I come to think of it,' Mrs Riversedge went on, 'there are things about Mr Brope that I've never been able to account for. His income, for instance: he only gets two hundred a year as editor of the *Cathedral Monthly*, and I know that his family is quite poor and that he hasn't any private source of income. Yet he manages to afford a flat somewhere in Westminster, and he goes abroad to Bruges and those sorts of places every year, and he always dresses well, and gives quite nice lunch-parties in the season. You can't do all that on two hundred pounds a year, can you?'

'Does he write for any other papers?' asked Mrs Troyle.

'No, you see he specializes so entirely on church services and religious architecture that his field is rather limited. He once sent a piece on church buildings in famous fox-hunting centres to *The Sporting and Dramatic Weekly*, but it wasn't considered of enough general interest to be accepted. No, I don't see how he can support himself in his present style just by what he writes.'

'Perhaps he sells bits of old church to American collectors,' suggested Clovis.

'How could you sell a bit of a church?' said Mrs Riversedge. 'Such a thing would be impossible.'

'Whatever he may do to increase his income,' interrupted Mrs Troyle, 'he's certainly not going to fill in his spare time by making love to my maid.'

'Of course not,' agreed her hostess. 'We must put a stop to that at once. But I don't quite know what we ought to do.'

'You might put a ring of wire round the lilac tree, as a first preventive step,' said Clovis.

'I don't think that this disagreeable situation is improved by sarcastic remarks,' said Mrs Riversedge. 'A good maid is worth her weight in gold, and –'

'I am sure I don't know what I should do without Florinda,' admitted Mrs Troyle. 'She understands my hair. I've long ago given up trying to do anything with it myself. I regard hair as I regard husbands: as long as one is seen together in public, one's differences in private don't matter . . . Surely that was the bell for lunch.'

Septimus Brope and Clovis had the smoking-room to themselves after lunch. The former seemed restless and uncomfortable, the latter quietly observant.

'What is a lory?' asked Septimus suddenly. 'I don't mean the thing on wheels, of course I know what that is; but isn't there a bird with a name like that – a sort of parrot?'

'I believe there is – but it's a "lory" with one "r",' said Clovis lazily, 'in which case it's no good to you.'

Septimus Brope looked at him in some astonishment. 'How do you mean, no good to me?' he asked, with more than a little uneasiness in his voice.

'It won't **rhyme** with Florrie,' explained Clovis.

Septimus sat upright in his chair, with unmistakable alarm on his face.

'How did you find out? I mean, how did you know I was trying to get a rhyme for Florrie?' he asked sharply.

'I didn't know,' said Clovis, 'I only guessed. When you wanted to turn a four-wheeled heavy goods vehicle into a beautiful bird flying among the leaves of a Brazilian forest, I knew that you must be working on a poem, and Florrie is the only female name that suggested itself as rhyming with lorry.'

Septimus still looked uneasy. 'I believe you know more,' he said.

Clovis laughed quietly, but said nothing.

'How much do you know?' asked Septimus desperately.

'The lilac tree in the garden,' said Clovis.

'There! I felt certain I'd dropped it somewhere. But you must have guessed something before. Look here, you've surprised my secret. You won't tell anyone, will you? It's nothing to be ashamed of, but, if people know that the editor of the *Cathedral Monthly* goes in for that sort of thing, it might give the wrong impression.'

'I suppose so,' admitted Clovis.

'You see,' continued Septimus, 'I get quite a lot of money out of it. I could never live in the style I do on what I earn as editor of the *Cathedral Monthly*.'

Clovis was even more astonished than Septimus had been earlier in the conversation, but he was more skilled at hiding his surprise. 'Do you mean to say you get money out of . . . Florrie?' he asked.

'Not out of Florrie, as yet,' said Septimus. 'In fact, I don't mind saying that I'm having a fair amount of trouble with Florrie. But there are a lot of others.'

Clovis's cigarette went out. 'This is very interesting,' he said slowly. And then, with Septimus Brope's next words, the truth became clear to him.

'There are plenty of others. For instance:

> Amy take me in your arms,
> Amaze me with your magic charms.

That was one of my earlier successes, and it still pays quite well. And then there is "Kitty, please take pity" and "Teresa, how I love to please her". Both of those have been fairly popular. And there is one rather awful one,' continued Septimus, turning deep red, 'which has brought me in more money than any of the others:

> Dear little Rose
> With her turned-up nose.

Of course I hate the whole lot of them; in fact I'm rapidly becoming something of a woman-hater under their influence, but I can't afford to ignore the financial returns from all this. And at the same time, you can understand that my

27

position as an authority on religious architecture and forms of church service would be weakened, if not completely ruined, if people found out that I was the author of "Amy take me in your arms" and all the rest of them.'

Clovis had recovered enough by now to ask in a sympathetic, if rather unsteady voice, what was the special trouble with 'Florrie'.

'I just can't get her into something easy to sing, however hard I try,' said Septimus gloomily. 'You see, one has to combine a lot of romantic, sugary compliments with a good rhyme, and a certain amount of lively personal description. They've all got to have a long string of past successes mentioned; or else you've got to suggest a future of perfect happiness for them and yourself. For instance, there is:

> Dearest, sweetest, little Glynis,
> How delicate and pure your chin is!
> All the money I can win is
> All to be for Glynis mine.

It goes to a sickly slow dance tune, and for months nothing else has been sung and whistled in the dance-halls of Blackpool and other popular centres.'

This time Clovis's self-control broke down badly. 'Please excuse me,' he managed to gasp out, 'but I can't help remembering the awful solemnity of that talk of yours that you so kindly gave us last night, on the Coptic tradition and its relation to Early Church history.'

Septimus sighed deeply. 'You see how it would be,' he said. 'As soon as people knew me to be the author of all that miserable romantic rubbish, all respect for the serious purpose of my life would be gone. I dare say I know more about church silver than anyone living, in fact I hope one day to write a book on the subject; but I should be

28

recognized as the man whose words were in the mouths of popular singers at every seaside town in the country. Can you be surprised that I positively hate Florrie, all the time that I've been trying to turn out sugar-coated songs about her?'

'Why not give free expression to your feelings and be thoroughly rude for a change? A song of complaint would have an instant success just because it would be different – but you would have to make it properly insulting.'

'I've never thought of that,' said Septimus, 'but I'm afraid I couldn't break away from my habit of romantic flattery and suddenly change my style.'

'You needn't change your style in the least,' said Clovis. 'Just change the feelings and keep to the same silly phrases. If you do the main part of the song, I'll do the **refrain**, which is the part that matters most, I believe. I shall want a half-share of all the money that it makes, and offer you my silence about your guilty secret for free. In the eyes of the world, you'll still be the man who has spent his whole life in the study of doorways and columns and Byzantine church ceremonies; only sometimes, in the long winter evenings, when the wind whistles icily down the chimney and the rain beats against the windows, I shall think of you as the author of "Amy come into my arms". Of course, if you feel grateful enough for my silence and would like to take me for a much-needed holiday on the Adriatic coast or somewhere equally interesting, I shouldn't dream of refusing.'

Later in the afternoon, Clovis found his aunt and Mrs Riversedge taking some gentle exercise in the rose garden. 'I've spoken to Mr Brope about F.,' he announced.

'How splendid of you! What did he say?' the two ladies replied with one voice.

'He was quite open with me when he saw that I knew his secret,' said Clovis, 'and it seems that his intentions were quite serious. I tried to show him what an impractical course he was following. He said he wanted to be understood, and he seemed to think that Florinda would do that to perfection; but I pointed out that there were probably dozens of well-brought-up, pure-hearted young English girls who would be able to understand him, while Florinda was the only person in the world who understood my aunt's hair. That made an impression on him, because he's not really a selfish animal, if you handle him correctly. And when I reminded him of his happy childhood days spent in the flowery fields of Leighton Buzzard (I suppose that flowers do grow there), he was obviously deeply moved. Anyhow, he gave me his word that he would put Florinda right out of his mind, and he has agreed to go for a short trip abroad as the best way to forget about the recent past. I am going with him as far as Ragusa. If my aunt should wish to give me a really nice scarf-pin (to be chosen by myself), as a small recognition of the very considerable service I have done her, I shouldn't dream of refusing. I'm not one of those people who think that, just because one is abroad, one can go about dressed in any old way.'

A few weeks later in Blackpool and other centres of popular song, the following refrain was on everybody's lips:

> How you bore me, Florrie,
> With those eyes of vacant blue.
> You'll be very sorry, Florrie,
> If I marry you.
> Though I'm easy going, Florrie,
> This I swear is true:
> I'll push you 'neath a lorry, Florrie,
> If I marry you.

# The Prize Pig

'There's a back way into the garden,' said Mrs Philidore Stossen to her daughter, 'through a small grass enclosure, and then through a walled kitchen garden full of **gooseberry** bushes. I went all over the place last summer when the family was away. There's a door that opens from the kitchen garden into the bushes at the far end of the main garden; and once we walk past those, we can mix with the guests as if we had come in the ordinary way. It's much safer than going in by the front entrance and running the risk of coming straight up against the hostess; that would be so awkward when she hasn't actually invited us.'

'Isn't it a lot of trouble to take for getting into a garden party?'

'To a garden party, yes. To *the* garden party of the season, certainly not. Everyone of any importance in the district, with the exception of ourselves, has been asked to meet the princess, and it would be far more trouble to invent explanations as to why we weren't there than to get in by an indirect route. I stopped Mrs Cuvering in the road yesterday and talked very pointedly about the princess. If she didn't take the hint and send me an invitation, it's not my fault, is it? Here we are: we just cut across the grass here and through that little gate into the garden.'

Mrs Stossen and her daughter, suitably dressed up for a country garden party with a princess as the chief guest, sailed through the narrow grass enclosure towards the gooseberry bushes with the air of warships advancing up a rural stream. There was a certain secretive hastiness mixed with the solemnity of their progress, as if enemy search-lights might be turned on them at any moment; and, as a matter of fact, they were not unobserved. Matilda Cuvering, with the sharp eyes of thirteen years and the added advantage of a look-out position in the branches of an apple tree, had enjoyed a good view of the Stossens' side approach and could see exactly where their plan would fail.

'They'll find the door out of the walled garden locked, and they'll just have to go back the way they came,' she remarked to herself. 'It's their own fault for not coming in by the proper entrance. What a pity Tarquin Superbus isn't loose in the field. After all, everyone else is enjoying themselves, I don't see why Tarquin shouldn't have an afternoon out.'

Matilda was of an age when thought is action. She slid down from the branches of the apple tree, and when she climbed back up again, Tarquin, the huge white Yorkshire male pig, had exchanged the narrow limits of his pig-house for the wider spaces of the grassy enclosure. The unsuccessful Stossen expedition, returning in good order but some annoyance from the barrier of the locked door, came to a sudden stop at the gate which divided the enclosure from the gooseberry garden.

'What an evil-looking animal,' exclaimed Mrs Stossen. 'It wasn't there when we came in.'

'It's there now, anyhow,' said her daughter. 'What on earth are we to do? I wish we had never come.'

The great pig had come nearer to the gate for a closer inspection of these unwelcome humans, and stood baring his teeth and opening and shutting his small red eyes in a manner that was doubtless intended to unsettle them; as far as the Stossens were concerned, it achieved that result very well indeed.

'Shoo! Hish! Hish! Shoo!' cried the ladies, keeping perfect time.

'If they think they're going to drive him away by shouting out lists of the Kings of Israel, they're going to be disappointed,' remarked Matilda from her seat in the apple

*The great pig had come nearer to the gate for a closer inspection
of these unwelcome humans, and stood baring his teeth.*

tree. As she made the remark aloud, Mrs Stossen became aware of her presence for the first time. A moment or two earlier, she would have been anything but pleased at the discovery that the garden was not as deserted as it looked, but now she accepted the fact of the child's presence on the scene with absolute relief.

'Little girl, can you find someone to drive away –' she began hopefully.

'*Comment? Comprends pas,*' was the reply.

'Oh, are you French? *Êtes-vous française?*'

'*Pas de tout, 'Suis anglaise.*'

'Then why not talk English? I want to know if –'

'*Permettez-moi expliquer* – let me explain. You see, I'm being punished,' said Matilda. 'I'm staying with my aunt and I was told I must behave particularly well today, as lots of people were coming for a garden party, and I was to imitate Claude – that's my younger cousin – who never does anything wrong except by accident, and then always apologizes for it. It seems that I ate too much gooseberry cream pudding at lunch and they said Claude never eats so much gooseberry pudding. Well, Claude always goes to sleep for half an hour after lunch, because he's told to, and I waited until he was asleep and tied his hands together and started feeding him by force with a whole bucketful of gooseberry cream that they were keeping for the garden party. Lots of it went down his sailor-suit and some of it went on to the bed, but a lot went down Claude's throat, and now they can't say that he has never eaten too much gooseberry cream. That's why I am not allowed to go to the garden party, and as an additional punishment I must speak French all the afternoon. I've had to tell you all this in English, as there are words I don't know the French for. I could have invented them, but you wouldn't have had the least idea what I was talking about. But now we must speak French – *maintenant nous parlons français.*'

'Oh, very well, *très bien,*' said Mrs Stossen unwillingly. In anxious moments the small amount of French she knew was not under very good control. *Là, à l'autre côté de la porte, est un cochon* – a pig . . .'

'*Un cochon? Ah, le petit charmant!*' exclaimed Matilda with enthusiasm.

'Small? Charming? *Mais non, pas du tout petit, et pas du tout charmant, un bête féroce –*'

'*Une bête,*' corrected Matilda. 'A pig is masculine as long as you call it a pig; but if you lose your temper and call it a fierce **beast**, it becomes one of us at once. French is a terribly confusing language.'

'For goodness' sake, let's talk English, then,' said Mrs Stossen. 'Is there any way out of this garden, except through the field where the pig is?'

'I always go over the wall by way of that fruit tree,' said Matilda.

'Dressed as we are, we could hardly do that,' said Mrs Stossen. It was difficult to imagine her doing it in any costume.

'Do you think you could go and get someone who would drive the pig away?' asked Mrs Stossen.

'I promised my aunt I would stay here until five o'clock. It's not four yet.'

'I'm sure, under the circumstances, your aunt would allow –'

'My conscience would not allow,' said Matilda coldly.

'We can't stay here until five o'clock,' exclaimed Mrs Stossen with a growing feeling of annoyance and helplessness.

'Shall I deliver a poem or two to make the time pass quicker?' asked Matilda innocently. '"Belinda the Little

Breadwinner" is considered to be my best piece; or perhaps it ought to be something in French. Henry the Fourth's speech to his soldiers is the only thing I really know in that language.'

'If you will go and fetch someone to drive that animal away, I will give you something to buy yourself a nice present,' said Mrs Stossen.

Matilda came several inches lower down the apple tree. 'That's the most practical suggestion you've made yet for getting out of the garden,' she remarked cheerfully. 'Claude and I are collecting money for the Children's Fresh Air Society and we're seeing which of us can collect the most.'

'I shall be very glad to let you have two **shillings** and sixpence, very glad indeed,' said Mrs Stossen, digging that amount out of the bottom of a handbag that formed an outer part of her costume.

'Claude is a long way ahead of me at present,' continued Matilda, taking no notice of the suggested offering. 'You see, he's only eleven, and has golden hair, and those are enormous advantages when you're on a collecting job. Only the other day a Russian lady gave him ten shillings. Russians understand the art of giving far better than we do. I expect Claude will collect a good twenty-five shillings this afternoon. He'll have no competition from me, and he'll be able to play the pale, delicate, not-long-for-this-world role to perfection, after his gooseberry cream experience. Yes, he'll certainly be two pounds ahead of me by now.'

With much seeking and searching and many regretful murmurs, the hard-pressed ladies managed to produce seven shillings and sixpence between them.

'I'm afraid this is all we've got,' said Mrs Stossen.

Matilda showed no sign of coming down either to the

ground or to the sum mentioned. 'I could not do violence to my conscience for anything less than ten shillings,' she announced stiffly.

Mother and daughter made certain remarks under their breath in which the word 'beast' appeared frequently, and probably did not refer to Tarquin.

'I find I *have* got another two and sixpence,' said Mrs Stossen in a shaking voice. 'Here you are. Now please fetch someone quickly.'

Matilda slipped down from the tree, took possession of the money, and paused to pick up a handful of overripe apples from the grass at her feet. Then she climbed over the gate and spoke affectionately to the pig.

'Come on, Tarquin, dear old boy. You know you can't resist apples when they're all rotten and squashy.'

Tarquin couldn't. By means of throwing the fruit in front of him at well-calculated intervals, Matilda led him back to the pig-house, while the prisoners, set free at last, hurried across the field.

'Well I never! The little devil!' exclaimed Mrs Stossen, when she was safely on the main road. 'The animal wasn't dangerous at all, and, as for our ten shillings, I don't believe the Fresh Air Society will see a penny of it!'

There she was unnecessarily severe in her judgement. If you examine the Society's records, you will find the words: 'Collected by Miss Matilda Cuvering: two shillings and sixpence.'

# The Outsiders

In a forest on the eastern edge of the Carpathian mountains, a man stood one winter night watching and listening, as though he were waiting for some wild animal of the woods to come within range of first his eyes and then his shotgun. But the kind of animal for which he was watching and waiting was not one which appeared in the sportsman's calendar as a lawful and proper object for hunting. Ulrich von Gradwitz stood guarding the dark forest in wait for a human enemy.

The forest lands of Gradwitz were large and well provided with **deer**; the narrow piece of steep woodland that lay at its outer edge was not remarkable for the amount of wildlife it contained or for the shooting it provided, but it was the most jealously guarded of all its owner's lands. A famous court-case in the time of his grandfather had recovered it from the illegal possession of a neighbouring family of small landowners. The losers of the land had never accepted the judgement of the courts, and a long series of deer-stealing and other crimes had soured the relationship between the two families since his grandfather's time. The quarrel with his neighbour had grown into a personal one since Ulrich had become head of the family: if there was one man in the world whom he hated and cursed it was Georg Znaeym, who had continued the quarrel and who constantly entered and shot animals in the border-forest area. The tradition of quarrelling between the two families might perhaps have died down or been settled if the personal hatred between the two men had not stood in the way. As boys, they had thirsted for one another's blood, and each still prayed that misfortune might fall on the other.

On this windswept winter night, Ulrich had called together his foresters to watch the dark forest, not in search of four-footed beasts, but to keep a look-out for the skilful thieves whom he suspected of crossing the land boundary. The deer, which usually kept to the sheltered hollow places during a storm, were running like driven things tonight, and there was movement and unrest among the forest creatures that were usually asleep during the dark hours. Undoubtedly there was a disturbing presence in the forest tonight, and Ulrich could guess what it was.

He wandered away by himself from the watchers whom he had placed in hiding on the top of the hill, and made his way far down the steep slopes among the thick mass of bushes, looking between the tree-trunks and listening through the whistling and sighing of the wind and the restless beating of branches for sight or sound of the robbers. If only on this wild night, in this dark, isolated place, he might come across Georg Znaeym man to man, without witnesses – that was the wish that ruled his thoughts. And as he stepped round the trunk of a huge, spreading tree, he came face to face with the man he was seeking.

The two enemies stood looking in anger at each other for a long, silent moment. Each had a shotgun in his hand, each had hate in his heart and murder in his mind. The chance had come to release the violent emotions of a lifetime. But a man who has been brought up under the rules of a higher civilization cannot easily force himself to shoot down his neighbour in cold blood and without a word spoken, except for an offence against his family and his good name. And, before the moment of hesitation had led to action, Nature's own violence overtook them both. The fierce roar of the storm had been answered by a loud crack over their heads, and, before they could leap aside, the mass of the tree had fallen on them like thunder. Ulrich von Gradwitz found himself stretched on the ground, with one arm crushed beneath him and the other held almost as helplessly by a confused pile of forked branches, while both legs were pinned beneath the fallen mass. It was clear that he could not move from his present position until someone came to release him. The falling branches had torn the skin of his face, and he had to shake off some drops of blood from his eyelids before he could see clearly what had happened. At his side, so near that under ordinary circumstances he could have touched him, lay Georg Znaeym, alive and struggling but obviously as helplessly pinned down as himself. All round them lay the wreck of the great tree in a heap of bent and broken branches.

Relief at being alive and anger at his helplessness brought a strange mixture of thank-offerings and curses to Ulrich's lips. Georg, who was nearly blinded with the blood which flowed across his eyes, stopped his struggling for a moment to listen, and then gave a short, bitter laugh.

'So you're not dead as you ought to be, but you're caught anyway,' he cried, 'caught like a rat! Oh, what a joke! Ulrich von Gradwitz trapped in his stolen forest. There's the hand of God at work!' And he laughed again, making cruel fun of his enemy's helplessness.

'I'm caught in my own forest-land,' answered Ulrich with spirit. 'When my men come to release us, you will wish perhaps that you had not been caught openly stealing deer on a neighbour's land. Have you no shame?'

Georg was silent for a moment; then he answered quietly: 'Are you sure that your men will find much to release? I have men too in the forest tonight, close behind me, and *they* will be here first and do the releasing. When they drag me out from under these cursed branches, it won't need much clumsiness on their part to roll this tree-trunk right over on top of you. Your men will find you dead under a fallen tree. As a formality, I shall send a letter of sympathy to your family.'

'It's a useful hint,' said Ulrich fiercely. 'My men have orders to follow me in ten minutes' time, seven of which must have passed already, and when they get me out . . . I will gladly remember your idea. Only, as you will have met your death while entering my lands illegally, I don't think a letter of sympathy to your family would be necessary.'

'Good,' roared Georg, 'good. We'll fight this quarrel out to the death, you and I and the foresters, with no cursed outsiders to come between us. Go straight to hell, Ulrich von Gradwitz!'

'The same to you, Georg Znaeym, you thieving dog!'

Both men spoke with the bitterness of possible defeat before them, for each knew that it might be a long time before his men would look for him or find him; it was a matter of pure chance which group would arrive first on the scene.

Both had now given up the useless struggle to free themselves from the mass of wood that held them down; Ulrich limited his efforts to bringing his one partly free arm near enough to his outer coat-pocket to take out his wine bottle. Even when he had done that, it was a long time before he could manage to unscrew the top or get any of the liquid down his throat. But what a heaven-sent drink it seemed. It was a mild winter, and little snow had fallen as yet, so the two imprisoned men suffered less from the cold than might have been the case at that season of the year. Nevertheless, the wine was warming and refreshing to the wounded man, and he looked across with something like a stab of pity to where his enemy lay, just keeping the cries of pain and exhaustion from crossing his lips.

'Could you reach this bottle if I threw it over to you?' asked Ulrich suddenly. 'There's good wine in it, and one may as well be as comfortable as one can. Let us drink, even if tonight one of us has to die.'

*Ulrich was silent for a few minutes, and lay listening to the endless whistling of the wind. An idea was slowly forming in his mind.*

'No, I can scarcely see anything, there's so much dried blood around my eyes,' said Georg. 'And in any case I don't drink wine with an enemy.'

Ulrich was silent for a few minutes, and lay listening to the endless whistling of the wind. An idea was slowly forming in his mind, an idea that gained strength every time that he looked across at the man who was fighting so stubbornly against pain and exhaustion. In the pain and weakness that Ulrich himself was feeling, the old fierce hatred seemed to be dying down.

'Neighbour,' he said after a while, 'do as you please if your men get here first. It was a fair agreement. But, as for me, I have changed my mind. If my men are the first to come, you shall be the first to be helped, as though you were my guest. We've quarrelled like devils all our lives over this stupid strip of forest, where the trees can't even stand upright in a breath of wind. Lying here tonight, thinking, I've come to realize we've been a pair of fools; there are better things in life than winning an argument over frontiers. Neighbour, if you'll help me to bury the old quarrel, I – I'll ask you to be my friend.'

Georg Znaeym was silent for so long that Ulrich thought perhaps he had fainted with the pain of his injuries. Then he spoke slowly, with long pauses.

'How amazed the whole district would be if we rode into the market square together. No one still living can remember seeing a Znaeym and a von Gradwitz talking to one another in friendship. And what peace there would be among our foresters if we ended our long war tonight. And if we chose to make peace among our people, there's no one who could interfere, no outsiders to break the peace . . . You would spend Sylvester night beneath my roof; and I would come and celebrate some festival at your castle . . . I could never fire a shot on your land, unless you invited me as a guest. And you would come and shoot with me down on the wetlands where the wild duck are. In all the countryside there are none that could oppose us if we wanted to make peace. I never thought that I would do anything but hate you all my life, but I think I've changed my mind about things too, this last half-hour. And you offered me your wine bottle . . . Ulrich von Gradwitz, I will be your friend.'

For a time both men were silent, turning over in their minds the wonderful changes that this dramatic peace would bring. In the cold, gloomy forest, with the wind tearing in repeated bursts through the bare branches and whistling round the tree-trunks, they lay and waited for the help that would bring release and relief to each of them. And each prayed that his men might be the first to show respectful attention to the enemy who had become a friend.

Soon, as the wind dropped for a moment, Ulrich broke the silence.

'Let's shout for help,' he said. 'In this interval while the wind has stopped, our voices may carry a little way.'

'They won't carry far through the trees and bushes,' said Georg. 'but we can try. Together, then.'

The two raised their voices in a long hunting-call.

'Together again,' said Ulrich, a few minutes later, after listening with total concentration for an answering shout.

'I heard something that time, I think,' said Ulrich.

'I heard nothing but the cursed wind,' said Georg, in a voice rough with strain.

There was silence again for some minutes, and then Ulrich gave a joyful cry.

'I can see figures coming through the wood. They're following the way I took, coming down the hillside.'

Both men raised their voices in as loud a shout as they could manage.

'They've heard us! They've stopped. Now they've seen us. They're running down the hill towards us,' cried Ulrich.

'How many of them are there?' asked Georg.

'I can't see distinctly,' said Ulrich. 'Nine or ten.'

'Then they're yours,' said Georg. 'I had only seven out with me.'

'They're making all the speed they can, brave boys,' said Ulrich gladly.

'Are they your men?' asked Georg. 'Are they your men?' he repeated impatiently, as Ulrich did not answer.

'No,' said Ulrich with a laugh – the mad, uncontrollable laugh of a man unnerved by horrible fear.

'Who are they?' asked Georg quickly, straining his eyes to see what the other would gladly not have seen.

'**Wolves**.'


## Tea

James Cushat-Prinkly was a young man who had always been quite sure that one of these days he would marry; up to the age of thirty-four he had done nothing to put this belief into action. He liked and admired a great many women collectively and from a distance, without choosing any one of them for special consideration regarding marriage, just as one might admire the Alps without feeling that one wanted any particular mountain as one's private property. His failure to act in this matter caused a certain amount of impatience among the romantically minded women of his home circle: his mother, his sisters, his resident aunts and two or three close middle-aged friends considered his delay in the question of marriage with a disapproval which was anything but silent. His innocently playful relationships were watched with the same eagerness which a group of restless dogs shows in following every movement of a human being who might reasonably be expected to take them for a walk. No one with normal feelings can resist for long the begging looks of several pairs of dogs' eyes.

James Cushat-Prinkly was not too strong-minded or unresponsive towards home influences to ignore the clearly expressed wish of his family that he should fall in love with some marriageable girl, and when his Uncle Jules died and left him a large sum of money, it really seemed the correct thing to do to discover someone else to share it with him. His search was guided more by his family's suggestions and the weight of public opinion than by any clear ideas of his own. A majority of his female relations and friends had already picked out Joan Sebastable as the most suitable young woman to receive his proposal of marriage, and James gradually got used to the idea that he and Joan would go together through the necessary stages of congratulations, receiving presents, a hotel in Norway or the Mediterranean and, finally, domestic life. It was first necessary, however, to ask the lady herself what she thought about the matter. The family had so far directed the whole affair with skill and good manners, but the actual proposal would have to be an individual effort.

Cushat-Prinkly walked across the park to the Sebastable home feeling fairly pleased with events. As the thing had to be done, he was glad to feel that he would get it all settled and off his mind that afternoon. Proposing marriage, even to a nice girl like Joan, was a rather boring business, but he could not have a holiday in Minorca and a future life of married happiness without such a ceremony first. He wondered what Minorca was really like as a place to stay in. In his mind's eye, it was an island with black or white

Minorca chickens running all over it, but probably it would not be at all like that.

His thoughts about the Mediterranean were interrupted by the sound of a clock striking the half-hour. Half past four. Lines of dissatisfaction settled on his face. He would arrive at the Sebastable household just at the hour of afternoon tea. Joan would be sitting at a low table, spread with a fine display of silver kettles and cream-jugs and delicate teacups, and her voice would ring out pleasantly in a series of little friendly questions about weak or strong tea, how much, if any, sugar, milk, cream and so on. 'Is it one lump of sugar? I forgot. You do take milk, don't you? Would you like some more hot water, if it's too strong?'

Cushat-Prinkly had read about such things in dozens of novels, and hundreds of actual experiences had told him that they were true to life. Thousands of women, at this solemn afternoon hour, were sitting behind pretty teacups and silver teapots with their voices gently releasing a whole series of caring little questions. Cushat-Prinkly hated the whole system of afternoon tea. According to his theory of life, a woman should lie on a sofa, talking with great charm, or looking as if her thoughts were too deep to be expressed, or simply keeping silent as something to be looked at; while from behind a silk curtain a little serving-boy should silently bring in cups and plates and delicious food, to be accepted silently, as a matter of course, without this endless discussion about cream and sugar and hot water. If one was really in love, how could one talk seriously about weakened tea? Cushat-Prinkly had never explained his views on this subject to his mother. All her life she had been in the habit of performing this ceremony behind the delicate pink and gold and silver of her tea-table, and if he had spoken to her about sofas, silk curtains and little serving-boys, she would have recommended him to take a week's holiday at the seaside.

Now, as he made his way through the small streets that led indirectly to the elegant Mayfair town house which was his destination, a horror at the idea of facing Joan Sebastable at her tea-table seized him. A temporary solution presented itself: on one floor of a narrow little house at the noisier end of Esquimault Street lived Rhoda Ellam, a sort of distant cousin, who made a living by creating hats out of expensive materials. The hats really looked as if they had come from Paris; the cheques she got for them unfortunately never looked so handsome. However, Rhoda appeared to find life amusing and to have a fairly good time, in spite of her modest circumstances. Cushat-Prinkly decided to climb up to her floor and postpone for half an hour or so the important business that lay before him. By extending his visit, he could reach the Sebastable household after the last cup and saucer had been cleared away.

Rhoda welcomed him into a room that seemed to serve as a workshop, sitting-room and kitchen combined, and to be wonderfully clean and comfortable at the same time.

'I'm having a picnic meal,' she announced. 'There's honey in that jar at your elbow. Begin on that brown bread and butter while I cut some more. Find yourself a cup; the teapot is behind you. Now tell me about hundreds of things.'

She made no other reference to food, but talked amusingly and made her visitor talk amusingly too. At the same time she prepared the bread and butter with masterly skill and produced slices of lemon, where so many women would simply have produced reasons and regrets for not having any. Cushat-Prinkly found that he was enjoying an excellent tea without having to answer as many questions about it as a Minister of Agriculture called on to reply during a national crisis caused by cattle disease.

'And now tell me why you've come to see me,' said Rhoda suddenly. 'You awake not only my curiosity but my business instincts. I hope you've come about hats. I heard the other day that someone had left you some money, and of course I thought it would be a wonderful idea for you to celebrate the event by buying beautiful, expensive hats for all your sisters. They may not have said anything about it, but I feel sure that the same idea has occurred to them. Of course, with the season of garden parties so close, I am rather rushed just now, but in my business we're accustomed to that.'

'I didn't come about hats,' said her visitor. 'In fact I don't think I really came about anything. I was passing and I just thought I'd look in and see you. Since I've been talking to you, however, a rather important idea has just come to me. If you'll forget about the garden parties for a moment and listen to me, I'll tell you what it is.'

Some forty minutes later, James Cushat-Prinkly returned to his eager family, bringing an important piece of news.

'I'm going to get married,' he announced.

A flood of congratulations and self-approval broke over him.

'Ah, we knew! We saw it coming! We guessed weeks ago it would happen!'

'I'll bet you didn't,' said Cushat-Prinkly. 'If anyone had told me at lunchtime today that I was going to ask Rhoda Ellam to marry me and that she was going to accept me, I would have laughed at the idea.'

The romantic suddenness of the affair in some way compensated James's female relations for the waste of all their patient efforts and skilful planning. It was rather awkward to have to direct their enthusiasm at a moment's notice away from Joan Sebastable to Rhoda Ellam; but, after all, it was James's wife who was in question, and it was only fair that his tastes should also be considered.

On a September afternoon of the same year, after their trip to Minorca, Cushat-Prinkly came into the sitting-room of his new house in Granchester Square. Rhoda was sitting at a low table behind a display of shining new teacups and a silver teapot. There was a pleasant, tender concern in her voice as she handed him a cup.

'You like it weaker than that, don't you? Shall I put some more hot water in it? No?'

## Mrs Packletide's Tiger

It was Mrs Packletide's pleasure and intention that she should shoot a tiger. It was not that a strong desire to kill had suddenly come over her, or that she felt that she would leave India safer and freer than she had found it, with one wild animal less to threaten its millions of inhabitants. The real motive of her sudden decision to take up hunting was the fact that Loona Bimberton had recently travelled eleven miles in an aeroplane with an Algerian pilot, and talked of nothing else. Only a tiger skin which she had obtained personally and a rich harvest of press photographs could successfully equal that sort of thing. Mrs Packletide had already arranged in her mind the lunch she would give at her house in Curzon Street, supposedly in Loona Bimberton's honour, with a tiger skin occupying most of the floor of the room and all of the conversation. She had also already designed in her mind the tiger-**claw** pin that she was going to give Loona Bimberton on her next birthday. In a world that is supposed to be moved by hunger and by love, Mrs Packletide was an exception: her movements and motives were largely determined by dislike of Loona Bimberton.

She was in luck. Mrs Packletide had offered a thousand **rupees** for the opportunity of shooting a tiger without too much risk or effort, and it so happened that a neighbouring village could claim to be the favourite feeding-ground of a respectable animal, which had been forced by old age to abandon killing wild beasts and limit its appetite to the smaller domestic animals. The thought of earning a thousand rupees had awakened the sporting and commercial instincts of the villagers. Children were sent to keep watch day and night on the edge of the local jungle to drive the tiger back if he should attempt to wander away to fresh hunting-grounds, and the cheaper kinds of **goat** were left around with calculated carelessness to keep him satisfied with his present home. The one great anxiety was that he might die of old age before the date fixed for the English lady's shoot. Mothers carrying their babies home through the jungle after their day's work in the fields stopped their singing in case it might cut short the restful sleep of the respected robber of their goats.

The great night finally arrived, moonlit and cloudless. A platform had been built in a comfortable and convenient tree, and on it sat Mrs Packletide and her paid companion, Miss Mebbin. A goat with an unusually loud cry, such as even a slightly deaf tiger might reasonably be expected to hear on a still night, was tied at the correct distance. With a good-quality shotgun and some playing-cards, the sportswoman waited for her victim to appear.

'I suppose we're in some danger?' said Miss Mebbin. She was not actually nervous about the wild beast, but she had a deep fear of performing the slightest service more than she had actually been paid for.

'Nonsense,' said Mrs Packletide. 'It's a very old tiger. It couldn't leap up here even if it wanted to.'

'If it's an old tiger, I think you ought to get it cheaper. A thousand rupees is a lot of money.'

Louisa Mebbin had a protective attitude towards money

in general, whether it was British or foreign. Her firm action had saved a lot of money from disappearing in the form of tips in a Moscow hotel; both notes and coins stuck close to her in circumstances which would have released them from less sympathetic hands.

Her thoughts about the market value of ageing tigers were cut short by the appearance on the scene of the animal itself. As soon as it caught sight of the tied-up goat, it lay flat on the ground, less, it seemed, from a wish to remain hidden than for the purpose of taking a short rest before it began the great attack.

'I believe it's ill,' said Louisa Mebbin loudly in Hindustani, for the benefit of the village headman, who was hiding in a neighbouring tree.

'Be quiet!' said Mrs Packletide, and at that moment the tiger began walking slowly towards its victim.

'Now! Now!' whispered Miss Mebbin urgently, in some excitement. 'If he doesn't touch the goat, we needn't pay for it.' (The goat cost extra.)

The shotgun flashed with a loud bang, and the great striped beast leapt to one side and then rolled over in the stillness of death. In a moment, a crowd of excited villagers had rushed on to the scene, and their shouting quickly carried the good news to the village, where a wild beating of drums took up the song of victory. Their joy found a ready echo in the heart of Mrs Packletide; already that lunch party in Curzon Street seemed very much nearer.

It was Louisa Mebbin who drew attention to the fact that the goat was dying slowly from a severe bullet-wound, while no sign of the shotgun's deadly work could be found on the tiger. Clearly the wrong animal had been hit, and the dangerous beast had died of heart failure, caused by the sudden noise of the shotgun, and helped along by old age. Mrs Packletide was understandably annoyed at this

*The shotgun flashed with a loud bang, and the great striped beast leapt to one side and then rolled over in the stillness of death.*

discovery; but at least she was now the owner of a dead tiger, and the villagers, anxious for their thousand rupees, gladly shared in the pretence that she had shot the beast. And Miss Mebbin was a paid companion.

So Mrs Packletide faced the cameras with a light heart, and her fame in pictures reached from the *Texas Picture Weekly* to the illustrated Monday issue of the Russian *Novoe Vremya*. As for Loona Bimberton, she refused to look at an illustrated paper for weeks, and her letter of thanks for the gift of a tiger-claw pin was a model of tightly controlled emotions. She regretfully felt unable to attend the lunch party; there are limits beyond which tightly controlled emotions can become dangerous.

From Curzon Street, the tiger skin travelled down to the Manor House, where it was laid out on the floor and was inspected and admired by everyone in the district. It seemed quite right that Mrs Packletide should go to the Costume Ball dressed as Diana, Goddess of Hunting.

'How amused everyone would be if they knew what really happened,' said Louisa Mebbin, a few days after the Costume Ball.

'What do you mean?' asked Mrs Packletide quickly.

'How you shot the goat and frightened the tiger to death,' said Miss Mebbin, with a sweet little laugh.

'No one would believe it,' said Mrs Packletide, her face rapidly changing colour.

'Loona Bimberton would,' said Miss Mebbin.

Mrs Packletide's face remained an unattractive shade of greenish white. 'You surely wouldn't betray me?' she asked.

'I've seen a weekend cottage near Dorking that I should rather like to buy,' said Miss Mebbin, as if the two matters were quite unconnected. 'Six hundred and eighty pounds. It's quite a bargain, only I don't happen to have the money.'

♦

Louisa Mebbin's pretty weekend cottage, which she has named 'Shangri-La' in memory of her travels in India, is bright in summer-time with its garden full of tiger-**lilies**, and is the admiration of her friends. 'It's amazing how Louisa manages to afford it' is the general opinion.

Mrs Packletide has given up hunting large animals. 'There are so many unexpected costs' is what she tells those friends who ask why.


## The Seven Cream-Jugs


'I suppose that we shall never see Wilfrid Pigeoncote here, now that he is **heir** to a lot of money,' remarked Mrs Peter Pigeoncote regretfully to her husband.

'Well, we can hardly expect to,' he replied, 'seeing that we always discouraged him from coming to see us when he was a nobody. I don't think I've even seen him since he was a boy of twelve.'

'There was a reason for not wanting to develop the relationship,' said Mrs Peter. 'With that well-known weakness of his, he was not the sort of person one wanted in one's house.'

'Well, the weakness still exists, doesn't it?' said her husband. 'Or do you suppose that his character has been completely changed by the expectation of becoming so wealthy?'

'Oh, of course the problem is still there,' admitted the wife, 'but one would like to get to know the future head of the family, if only out of curiosity. Besides, now he's going to be rich, there will be a difference in the way people look at his weakness. When a man is really wealthy, not just well-off, any suspicion of dishonest motives naturally disappears; the thing becomes simply an unfortunate illness.'

Wilfrid Pigeoncote had suddenly become heir to his uncle, Sir Wilfrid Pigeoncote, on the death of his cousin, Major Wilfrid Pigeoncote, who had died as the result of a sporting accident. (A Wilfrid Pigeoncote had become quite famous in the wars of the eighteenth century, and the name Wilfrid had been preferred by the family ever since.) The new heir to the family wealth was a young man of about twenty-five, who was known more by reputation than in person to a wide circle of cousins and relatives. And this reputation was an unpleasant one. The numerous other Wilfrids in the family were usually known by the names of their homes or their professions, such as Wilfrid of Hubbledown, and young Wilfrid the Gunner; but this particular family member was known by the expressive label of Thieving Wilfrid. From his school-days onwards, he had suffered from a severe and stubborn desire to steal things, and he had all the energy of a great collector without any of a collector's fine judgement. Anything that was smaller and easier to remove than a piano, and with a value over ninepence, had an irresistible attraction for him, as long as it belonged to someone else. On the rare occasions when he was included in a country-house party, it was usual and almost necessary for his host, or some member of the family, to carry out a friendly search of his luggage the evening before his departure, to see if he had packed 'by mistake' anyone else's property. The search usually produced a large and varied collection.

'This is funny,' said Peter Pigeoncote to his wife, about half an hour after their conversation. 'Here's a telegram from Wilfrid, saying he's passing through here in his car, and would like to stop and pay us a visit. He can stay for the night if it's not inconvenient. Signed "Wilfrid Pigeoncote". It must be Thieving Wilfrid: none of the others has a car. I suppose he's bringing us a present for our silver wedding.'*

'Good heavens!' said Mrs Peter, as a thought came to her. 'This is rather an awkward time to have a person with his problem in the house: all those silver presents on display in the sitting-room and others coming in by every post. I hardly know what we've got and what is still to come. We can't lock them all up; he's sure to want to see them.'

'We must keep a sharp look-out, that's all,' said Peter, trying to calm her fears.

'But these people with an urge to steal are so clever,' said his wife anxiously, 'and it will be so awkward if he suspects that we are watching him.'

Awkwardness was indeed the main feeling that evening when the passing traveller was being entertained. The talk switched nervously and hurriedly from one impersonal topic to another. The guest had none of that suspicious air that his cousins had rather expected to find. He was polite, confident and perhaps just a little boastful. His hosts, on the other hand, displayed an uneasiness that seemed to suggest guilt. In the sitting-room after dinner, their nervousness and awkwardness increased.

'Oh, we haven't shown you the silver wedding presents,' said Mrs Peter, as though she had suddenly had a brilliant idea for entertaining the guest. 'Here they all are. Such nice useful gifts. A few items are repeated, of course.'

'Seven cream-jugs,' contributed Peter.

'Yes, isn't it annoying?' went on Mrs Peter, 'Seven of them. We feel that we must live on cream for the rest of our lives. Of course, some of them can be changed.'

* A silver wedding celebrates twenty-five years of married life.

Wilfrid studied mainly those gifts which had antique interest, carrying one or two of them over to the lamp to examine their marks. The anxiety of his hosts at these moments was like a cat whose newly born babies are being handed round for inspection.

'Let me see, did you give me back the mustard-pot? This is its place here,' said Mrs Peter firmly.

'Sorry. I put it down by the wine-jug,' said Wilfrid, busy with another object.

'Oh, just let me have that sugar-shaker again,' asked Mrs Peter, iron determination showing through her nervousness. 'I must label it with who it comes from before I forget.'

Their watchfulness was not completely rewarded with a sense of victory. After they had said good night to their visitor, Mrs Peter said she felt sure that he had taken something.

'I thought from his manner that something was going on,' agreed her husband. 'Do you miss anything?'

Mrs Peter hurriedly counted the display of gifts. 'I can only make it thirty-four and I think it should be thirty-five,' she announced. 'I can't remember if the thirty-five includes the general's cake-dish that hasn't arrived yet.'

'How on earth do we know?' said Peter. 'The selfish pig hasn't brought us a present, and I certainly won't let him carry one off.'

'Tomorrow, when he's having his bath,' said Mrs Peter excitedly. 'He's sure to leave his keys somewhere, and we can go through his suitcase. It's the only thing to do.'

The next day an alert watch was kept by the plotters behind half-closed doors, and when Wilfrid, splendidly dressed for his bath, had made his way to the bathroom, there was a quick, silent rush by two excited individuals towards the main guest bedroom. Mrs Peter kept guard outside while

*Mrs Peter kept guard outside while her husband searched for the keys and then dived at the suitcase with the air of a customs officer.*

her husband made a rapid and successful search for the keys and then dived at the suitcase with the air of an unpleasantly dutiful customs officer. The search did not take long: a silver cream-jug lay wrapped in the folds of some silk shirts.

'The tricky devil!' said Mrs Peter. 'He took a cream-jug because there were so many; he thought one wouldn't be missed. Quick, fly downstairs with it and put it back among the others.'

Wilfrid was late in coming down to breakfast, and his manner showed plainly that something was wrong.

'It's an unpleasant thing to have to say,' he said bluntly, 'but I'm afraid you must have a thief among your servants. Something's been taken out of my suitcase. It was a little present from my mother and myself for your silver wedding. I would have given it to you last night after dinner, but it happened to be a cream-jug, and you seemed annoyed at having so many of them, so I felt rather awkward about giving you another. I thought I'd get it changed for something else and now it's gone.'

'Did you say it was from your *mother* and yourself?' asked Mr and Mrs Peter, almost with one voice. Thieving Wilfrid had been an orphan for years.

'Yes, my mother's in Cairo just now and she wrote to me at Dresden to try to get you something pretty made of silver, so I decided on this cream-jug.'

Both the Pigeoncotes had turned deadly pale. The mention of Dresden had thrown a sudden light on the situation. It was Wilfrid of the Foreign Service, a very superior young man, who rarely came within their social horizon and whom they had been entertaining with the mistaken idea that he was Thieving Wilfrid. Lady Ernestine Pigeoncote, his mother, moved in circles which were entirely beyond their reach or social ambitions, and the son would probably one day be an ambassador. And they had searched his suitcase! Husband and wife looked blankly and desperately at each other. It was Mrs Peter who arrived first at a brilliant solution.

'How awful to think there are thieves in the house! We keep the sitting-room locked up at night, of course, but anything might be removed while we are at breakfast.'

She rose and went out hurriedly, as though to check that the sitting-room had not been stripped of its silver collection, and returned a moment later, carrying a cream-jug in her hands.

'There are eight cream-jugs now, instead of seven,' she cried.

'This one wasn't there before. What a curious trick of memory, Mr Wilfrid! You must have crept downstairs with it last night and put it there before we locked up, and forgotten all about having done it in the morning.'

'One's mind often plays little tricks like that,' said Mr Peter, with desperate hopefulness. 'Only the other day I went into town to pay a bill, and went in again the next day, having forgotten that I'd –'

'It's certainly the jug I bought for you,' said Wilfrid, looking closely at it. 'It was in my suitcase when I got dressed for my bath this morning, and it was not there when I unlocked the suitcase again on my return. Someone had taken it while I was out of the room.'

The Pigeoncotes had turned paler than ever. Mrs Peter had a final desperate idea.

'Get me my handbag, dear,' she said to her husband. 'I think it's in the dressing-room.'

Peter ran out of the room with relief: he had lived so long during the last few minutes that a golden wedding★ seemed within measurable distance.

★ A golden wedding celebrates fifty years of married life.

Mrs Peter turned to her guest with confidential shyness. 'A man of the world like you will know how to treat this as if it hadn't happened. It's Peter's little weakness, you know; it runs in the family.'

'Good God! Do you mean to say he suffers from the same problem as Thieving Wilfrid?'

'Oh, not exactly,' said Mrs Peter, anxious to make her husband look a little greyer than she was painting him. 'He would never touch anything that he found lying about; but he can't resist attacking things that are locked up. The doctors have a special name for it. He must have leapt on your suitcase the moment you went for your bath and taken the first thing he came across. Of course he had no motive for taking a cream-jug: we've already got *seven*, as you know – not, of course, that we don't value the kind gift which you and your mother – Quiet now, here's Peter coming.'

Mrs Peter broke off in some confusion and stepped out to meet her husband in the hall.

'It's all right,' she whispered to him. 'I've explained everything. Don't say anything more about it.'

'Brave little woman,' said Peter with a sigh of relief. 'I could never have done it.'

♦

The ability of even future ambassadors to keep silent about scandals does not necessarily extend to family affairs. Peter Pigeoncote was never able to understand why Mrs Consuelo van Bullyon, who stayed with them in the spring, always carried two very obvious jewel-cases with her to the bathroom, explaining them to anyone she happened to meet in the corridor as her special bath salts and her hairbrushes.

# Tobermory

It was a cold, rain-washed afternoon of a late August day when the season for shooting and hunting had not yet arrived, so Lady Blemley's house party had kept indoors. There was a full gathering of her guests round the tea-table on this particular afternoon. In spite of the quietness of the season and the familiarity of the occasion, there was no sign of the boredom and restlessness that means a demand for someone to play the piano or for card games to be organized.

The attention of the whole group was fixed on the modest, negative personality of Mr Cornelius Appin. Of all her guests, he was the one who had come to Lady Blemley with the least definite reputation. Someone had said he was 'clever', and he had been invited by his hostess in the hope that at least some of his cleverness would form part of the general entertainment. Until tea-time that day she had been unable to discover in what direction, if any, his cleverness lay. He was neither an amusing conversationalist nor a sports champion, nor good at organizing theatrical events. Nor did his appearance suggest the sort of man in whom women are willing to excuse a generous lack of brainpower. He had remained just Mr Appin, and the name Cornelius seemed little more than a trick of his parents to make him appear more interesting than he really was. But now he was claiming to have made a discovery beside which the invention of gunpowder, the printing-press and the steam-engine seemed rather minor events. Science had made astonishing advances in recent years, but his discovery seemed more unbelievable than any scientific achievement.

'And do you really ask us to believe,' Sir Wilfrid was saying, 'that you have discovered a way of teaching animals the art of human speech, and that dear old Tobermory has been your first successful pupil?'

'It is a problem which I have worked on for the last seventeen years,' said Mr Appin, 'but only in the last eight or nine months have I been rewarded with any sort of success. Of course I have experimented with thousands of animals, but lately only with cats, those wonderful creatures which have adjusted so well to our civilization while keeping all their highly developed instincts as wild animals. Here and there among cats one comes across an unusually brilliant mind, just as one does among the mass of human beings, and when I first got to know Tobermory a week ago, I saw at once that I was in contact with a "supercat" of extraordinary intelligence. I had gone far along the road to success in recent experiments: with Tobermory, as you call him, I have reached my goal.'

Mr Appin ended his remarkable statement in a voice which he tried to keep free of pride. No one said 'Rubbish', though Clovis's lips moved silently to pronounce that word.

'And do you mean to say,' said Miss Resker, after a slight pause, 'that you have taught Tobermory to say and understand one-word sentences?'

'My dear Miss Resker,' said the wonder-worker patiently, 'one teaches little children and unintelligent adults in that simplified fashion; when once one has solved the problem of how to approach an animal of highly developed intelligence, one has no need of such inefficient methods. Tobermory can speak our language with perfect correctness.'

This time Clovis very distinctly said 'Super-rubbish!' Sir Wilfrid was more polite but equally disbelieving.

'Hadn't we better have the cat in and judge for ourselves?' suggested Lady Blemley.

Sir Wilfrid went in search of the animal, and his group of guests settled down with the expectation of witnessing some more or less skilful trick of voice production, as a way of passing the time.

In a minute or two Sir Wilfrid was back in the room, his normally sunburnt face white and his eyes wide with excitement.

'By God, it's true!' His emotion was unmistakably real, and his hearers leant forward in a thrill of awakened interest.

Letting himself fall into an armchair, he continued breathlessly: 'I found him sleeping in the smoking-room and called out to him to come for his tea. He looked at me sleepily in his usual way, and I said, "Come on, Toby; don't keep us waiting," and, by God, he replied lazily in the most horribly natural voice that he'd come when it suited him and not before! I nearly jumped out of my skin!'

Appin had spoken to hearers who were deeply disbelieving; Sir Wilfrid's statement was accepted immediately. A flood of surprised comments broke out, in the centre of which the scientist sat silently enjoying the first results of his amazing discovery.

In the middle of the storm of voices, Tobermory stepped softly into the room and, seemingly with total lack of interest, made his way to the group sitting round the tea-table. A sudden uneasy quietness descended on the room. There seemed a feeling of embarrassment in the air at having to make conversation with a cat of superior mental ability.

'Will you have some milk, Tobermory?' asked Lady Blemley in a rather faint voice.

'I don't mind if I do,' was the reply, expressed in a voice of unmistakable boredom.

A wave of barely controlled excitement went through the listeners, and Lady Blemley could be forgiven for pouring out the saucerful of milk rather unsteadily.

'I'm afraid I've spilt a good deal of it,' she said.

'Will you have some milk, Tobermory?' asked Lady Blemley in
a rather faint voice.

'Well, it's your carpet, not mine,' was Tobermory's reply.

Another silence fell on the group, and then Miss Resker, with exaggerated politeness, asked if the human language had been difficult to learn. Tobermory looked directly at her and then fixed his eyes calmly on the middle distance. It was obvious that boring questions lay outside his scheme of life.

'What do you think of human intelligence?' asked Mavis Pellington, with a weak smile.

'Whose intelligence in particular?' asked Tobermory coldly.

'Oh, well, mine for example,' said Mavis with a foolish laugh.

'You put me in an embarrassing position,' said Tobermory, although his voice and manner did not betray the least sign of embarrassment. 'When it was suggested that you should be included in his house party, Sir Wilfrid protested that you were the most brainless woman he knew and that there was a big difference between hospitality and the care of the mentally backward. Lady Blemley replied that your lack of brainpower was exactly the quality which had earned you the invitation, as you were the only person who might be stupid enough to buy their old car. You know, the one which goes quite nicely uphill, provided you push it.'

Lady Blemley's protests would have had greater effect if she had not happened to suggest to Mavis only that morning that the car in question would be just the thing for her down at her Devonshire home.

Major Barfield bravely took over the interview to draw attention away from his hostess. 'How about your love affairs with the striped cat up at the farmhouse, eh?'

The moment he had said it, everyone realized his mistake.

'One does not usually discuss these matters in public,' said Tobermory in an icy voice. 'From my observation of your ways since you've been in this house, I should imagine that you would not enjoy my turning the conversation to the subject of your own little affairs.'

The alarm which followed was not felt only by the major.

'Would you like to go and see if cook has got your dinner ready?' suggested Lady Blemley hurriedly, pretending to ignore the fact that Tobermory's dinner-time was at least two hours away.

'Thanks', said Tobermory, 'not quite so soon after my tea. I don't want to die of indigestion.'

'Cats have nine lives, you know,' said Sir Wilfrid heartily.

'Possibly,' answered Tobermory, 'but only one **liver**.'

'Adelaide!' said Mrs Cornett, 'do you mean to encourage that cat to go out and tell stories about us in the servants' hall?'

The alarm had indeed become general. A narrow decorative rail ran in front of most of the bedroom windows at Blemley Towers, and people remembered with anxiety that this had been a favourite walk for Tobermory at all hours, from where he could watch the birds on the roof – and heaven knows what else besides. If he intended to describe some of his memories as freely as he was now speaking, the effect could be little less than disastrous. Mrs Cornett, who spent much of her time at her dressing-table and whose skin colour was thought to be artfully but artificially applied, looked just as uneasy as the major. Miss Scrawen, who wrote extremely exciting poems and led a blameless life, showed only annoyance: if your private life is cautious and highly respectable, you don't necessarily want everyone to know it. Bertie van Tahn, who at the age of seventeen was so wicked that he had long ago given up trying to be any worse, turned a dull shade of white; but he did not make the mistake of rushing from the room like Odo Finsberry, a young gentleman who was preparing to enter the Church and who was perhaps disturbed at the thought of the damaging remarks he might hear about other people. Clovis had the good sense to remain outwardly calm; privately he was estimating how long it would take to obtain a box of special mice with which to buy Tobermory's silence.

Even in a difficult situation like the present, Agnes Resker did not like to remain too long in the background. 'Why did I ever come down here?' she asked dramatically.

Tobermory immediately seized the opportunity. 'Judging by what you said to Mrs Cornett on the tennis-court yesterday, you came because of the food. You described the Blemleys as the dullest people to stay with that you knew, but said they were clever enough to employ a first-class cook; otherwise they'd find it difficult to get anyone to come down a second time.'

'There's not a word of truth in it! I ask Mrs Cornett to be my witness,' exclaimed Agnes in great embarrassment.

'Mrs Cornett repeated your remark afterwards to Bertie van Tahn,' continued Tobermory, 'and said, "That woman is as greedy as a pig: she'd go anywhere for four square meals a day", and Bertie van Tahn said –'

At this point the history of the house and its guests was mercifully interrupted. Tobermory had caught sight of the big yellow male cat from the doctor's house, working his way through the bushes towards the area where the horses were kept. In a flash Tobermory had disappeared through the open french window.

With the disappearance of his too-brilliant pupil, Cornelius Appin was met with a storm of bitter accusations, anxious questions and frightened requests. The responsibility for the situation lay with him, and he must prevent matters from becoming worse. Could Tobermory transfer his dangerous gift to other cats? was the first question he had to answer. It was possible, he replied, that he might have taught his new skill to his close friend, the cat at the farmyard; but it was unlikely that his teaching could have spread more widely just yet.

'Then,' said Mrs Cornett, 'Tobermory may be a valuable cat and a great pet, but I'm sure you'll agree, Adelaide, that both he and the farm cat must be destroyed without delay.'

'You don't suppose I've enjoyed the last quarter of an hour, do you?' said Lady Blemley bitterly. 'My husband and I are very fond of Tobermory – at least we were before this horrible skill was introduced into him; but now, of course, the only thing to do is to have him destroyed as soon as possible.'

'We can put some poison in the food he always gets at dinner-time,' said Sir Wilfrid, 'and I will go and drown the farm cat myself. The farmer will be very unhappy at losing his pet, but I'll say that a very infectious cat disease had been found in both cats and that we're afraid of it spreading to the dog population.'

'But my great discovery!' protested Mr Appin. 'After all my years of study and experiment –'

'You can go and experiment on the cows at the farm, which are under proper control,' said Mrs Cornett, 'or the elephants at the Zoological Gardens. They're said to be very intelligent, and they have this in their favour: they don't come creeping into our bedrooms and under chairs and so on.'

An angel announcing the End of the World, and then finding that the date was the same as the Oxford and

Cambridge Boat Race* and would have to be indefinitely postponed, could hardly have felt more disappointed than Cornelius Appin at the way his wonderful achievement had been received. Public opinion, however, was against him; in fact, if everybody in the house had been asked, it is probable that a strong minority would have voted in favour of poisoning him too.

Infrequent trains and a nervous desire to see matters brought to a finish prevented the guests from departing immediately, but dinner that evening was not a social success: Sir Wilfrid had rather a difficult time with the farm cat and later with the farmer himself. Agnes Resker pointedly limited her part in the meal to a small piece of dry toast, which she bit as though it was a personal enemy; while Mavis Pellington sat through the meal in bitter silence. Lady Blemley kept up a flow of what she hoped was conversation, but her attention was fixed on the doorway. A plateful of carefully prepared pieces of fish was kept ready on a side-table, but the various courses followed one another and no Tobermory appeared, either in the dining-room or the kitchen.

The gloomy dinner was cheerful compared with the endless watching and waiting later, in the smoking-room. Eating and drinking had at least supplied an activity and a cover of sorts for the general feeling of embarrassment. Card games were out of the question in the atmosphere of nerves and bad temper, and after Odo Finsberry had given a depressing performance of 'Mélisande in the Wood' to an unappreciative audience, everyone silently agreed that music would be out of place. At eleven, the servants went

* The Oxford and Cambridge Boat Race is a sporting event between rowing teams from the two universities which is held every year on the River Thames in London.

to bed, announcing that the small window in the back kitchen had been left open as usual for Tobermory's private use. The guests read steadily through all the current newspapers and were finally reduced to old copies of *Punch* magazine. Lady Blemley made periodic visits to the kitchen, returning each time with a look of depression on her face that discouraged any questions.

At two o'clock Clovis broke the universal silence. 'He won't come back tonight. He's probably in the local newspaper office at the present moment, giving a full account of his recent experiences to one of the reporters. Lady What's-her-name's book will seem quite dull by comparison. It'll be the event of the day.'

Having made this contribution to the general cheerfulness, Clovis went to bed. At long intervals the various members of the house party followed his example.

The servants taking round the early-morning tea gave everyone the same answer in reply to the same question: Tobermory had not returned.

Breakfast was, if anything, an even more unpleasant event than dinner had been, but, before it ended, relief arrived.

Tobermory's dead body was brought in from the bushes, where a gardener had just discovered it. From the bites on his throat and the yellow fur which filled his claws, it was clear that he had died in an unequal fight with the big male cat belonging to the local doctor.

By midday most of the guests had left Blemley Towers, and after lunch Lady Blemley had recovered enough to write an extremely nasty letter to the doctor about the loss of her valuable pet.

Tobermory had been Appin's one successful pupil, and he was to have no others. A few weeks later, an elephant in the Dresden Zoological Gardens, which had shown no previous signs of bad temper, broke loose and killed an Englishman who had apparently been annoying it. The victim's name was variously given in the newspapers as Oppin and Eppelin, but his first name was correctly stated to be Cornelius.

'If he was trying German irregular **verbs** on the poor creature,' said Clovis, 'he deserved all he got.'

## Dusk

Norman Gortsby sat on a bench in the park, with his back to a grassy strip planted with bushes, marked off by the boundary fence in front of him across a wide length of roadway. Hyde Park Corner, with the noise of its traffic, lay immediately to his right. It was about thirty minutes past six on an early March evening, and dusk had fallen heavily over the scene, dusk relieved by some faint moonlight and many street-lamps. There was a wide emptiness over the road and the pavement, and yet there were many shadowy figures moving silently through the half-light or sitting unobserved on benches and chairs, hardly distinct from the gloom in which they sat.

The scene pleased Gortsby and suited his present mood. Dusk, to his way of thinking, was the hour of the defeated. Men and women who had fought and lost, who hid their misfortunes and dead hopes as far as possible from the eyes of the curious, came out at this hour of dim light, when their old worn clothes, bowed shoulders and unhappy eyes could pass unnoticed, or at least unrecognized.

A King that is conquered must see strange looks
So bitter a thing is the heart of man.

The wanderers in the dusk did not wish to have strange looks fixed on them, so they came out like creatures of the night, taking their pleasure sadly in a pleasure-ground that had emptied of its normal occupants. Brilliant rows of windows shone through the dusk and almost cancelled it, marking the homes of those people who held themselves upright in life's struggle, or at least had not had to admit failure.

That is how Gortsby's imagination pictured things, as he sat on his bench in the almost empty walk. Money troubles did not press on him; if he had wished, he could have gone for a walk through the streets full of light and noise, and taken his place in the crowds of those who lived a comfortable life or who struggled to live one. He himself had failed in a less obvious way, and for the moment he was heavy-hearted and depressed, willing to take a certain pleasure in observing and labelling his fellow wanderers as they went their ways in the dark intervals between the lamplights.

On the bench by his side sat an elderly gentleman, who seemed, not quite successfully, to be putting on a brave face towards the world in spite of all his ill-luck. His clothes were just about acceptable, at least in the half-light, though it was difficult to imagine him buying a box of chocolates, or a flower for his buttonhole. He seemed one of the world's lonely people, whose sorrows meet with no response from others. As he got up to go, Gortsby imagined him returning to a home where he was treated without respect and generally ignored, or to some cheerless lodging-house where his ability to pay the weekly bill was the beginning and end of the interest people took in him. His figure, as he walked away, disappeared slowly in the shadows, and his place on the bench was taken almost immediately by a young man, fairly well-dressed but scarcely more cheerful-looking than the previous man had been. As if to underline the fact that he was in trouble, the newcomer swore angrily and loudly as he threw himself into the seat.

'You don't seem in a very good temper,' said Gortsby, understanding that he was expected to react in some way to this demonstration.

The young man turned to him with an eager openness which immediately made Gortsby cautious.

'You wouldn't be in a good temper if you were in the mess I'm in,' he said. 'I've done the silliest thing I've ever done in my life.'

'Yes?' said Gortsby, not wishing to be involved.

'I came up this afternoon, meaning to stay at the Patagonian Hotel in Berkshire Square,' continued the young man. 'When I got there, I found it had been pulled down some weeks ago and a cinema had been put up in its place. The taxi-driver recommended me to another hotel some way off and I went there. I just sent a letter to my family, giving them the address, and then I went out to buy some soap – I'd forgotten to pack any and I hate using hotel soap. Then I walked around for a bit, had a drink at a bar and looked at the shops and, when I came to make my way back to the hotel, I suddenly realized that I couldn't remember its name, or even what street it was in. There's a fine situation for someone who hasn't any friends or connections in London! Of course I can telephone to my family for the address, but they won't get my letter until tomorrow. Meanwhile I'm without any money – I came out with only a few coins in my pocket, which were spent in buying the soap and getting the drink; and here I am wandering about with twopence in my pocket and nowhere to go for the night.'

There was an expectant pause after the story had been told.

'I suppose you think I've invented the whole thing,' said the young man after a moment, with a hint of criticism in his voice.

'It's not at all impossible,' was Gortsby's carefully expressed opinion. 'I remember doing exactly the same thing once in a foreign capital, and on that occasion there were two of us, which made it all the more unusual. Luckily we remembered that the hotel was near a river, and when we came to the river we were able to find our way back to the hotel.'

The young man brightened up at this remark. 'In a foreign city I wouldn't mind so much,' he said. 'One could go to one's embassy and get the necessary help from there. Here, in one's own country, one is far more at a disadvantage if one gets into trouble. Unless I can find some kind-hearted person willing to accept my story and lend me some money, I seem likely to spend the night sleeping in the streets. I'm glad, anyhow, that you don't think the story completely improbable.' He made the last remark in a meaningful way, as if perhaps to indicate his hope that Gortsby's heart was sufficiently kind.

'Of course,' said Gortsby slowly, 'the weak point of your story is that you can't produce the soap.'

The young man sat forward hurriedly, felt rapidly in the pockets of his overcoat and then jumped to his feet. 'I must have lost it,' he said in a low, angry voice.

'To lose a hotel *and* a cake of soap on one afternoon suggests deliberate carelessness,' said Gortsby. But the young man scarcely waited to hear the end of the remark; he disappeared down the path, his head held confidently high but with a rather defeated air.

'It was a pity,' thought Gortsby. 'The going out to get one's own soap was the one realistic touch in the whole story, and yet it was that little detail that was his downfall.

If he had had the cleverness to provide himself with a cake of soap, newly wrapped from the chemist's, he would have succeeded brilliantly. In his particular game, success depends on paying attention to every detail.'

With these thoughts, Gortsby got up to go. As he did so, an exclamation of concern escaped him. Lying on the ground by the side of the bench was a small oval packet, newly wrapped by a chemist. It could be nothing else but a cake of soap, and it had obviously fallen out of the youth's overcoat pocket when he threw himself down on the seat. In another moment Gortsby was hurrying along the dusky path in anxious search of a youthful figure in a light overcoat. He had nearly given up the search when he caught sight of him, standing indecisively at the edge of the roadway, clearly uncertain whether to set out across the park or make for the crowded pavements of Knightsbridge. He turned round sharply with an unfriendly, defensive expression when he heard Gortsby calling him.

'The key witness to the truth of your story has appeared,' said Gortsby, holding out the cake of soap. 'It must have fallen out of your overcoat pocket when you sat down on the seat. I saw it on the ground after you left. You must excuse my disbelief, but appearances were rather against you; and now I think I should respect the evidence. If the loan of a couple of pounds is any good to you –'

The young man quickly removed all doubt on the subject by pocketing the money.

'Here is my card with my address,' continued Gortsby. 'Any day this week will do for returning the money. And here is the soap – don't lose it again, it's been a good friend to you.'

'Lucky that you found it,' said the youth, and then, with a tremble in his voice, he murmured a word or two of thanks and ran off in the direction of Knightsbridge.

'Poor boy, he was almost in tears,' said Gortsby to himself. 'I don't wonder either; the relief from overcoming such a difficulty must have been enormous. It's a lesson to me not to be too clever in judging by circumstances.'

As Gortsby walked past the seat where the little drama had taken place, he saw an elderly gentleman searching beneath it and on all sides of it, and recognized his earlier companion.

'Have you lost anything, sir?' he asked.

'Yes, sir, a cake of soap.'

## The Lumber-Room

The children were to be taken on a special outing to the sands at Jagborough. Nicholas was not included: he was being punished. Only that morning he had refused to eat his bread and milk for the seemingly stupid reason that there was a **frog** in it. Older and wiser and better people had told him that there could not possibly be a frog in his bread and milk and that he was not to talk nonsense. Nevertheless he continued to talk what seemed absolute nonsense, and described in great detail the colours and markings of the supposed frog. The dramatic part of it was that there really was a frog in Nicholas's bowl of bread and milk. He had put it there himself, so he felt he had the right to know something about it. The crime of taking a frog from the garden and putting it into a bowl of health-giving bread and milk was analysed at great length, but the fact that stood out most clearly in the whole business, as Nicholas saw it, was that the older, wiser and better people had been shown to be quite wrong in matters about which they had claimed to know everything.

'You said there couldn't possibly be a frog in my bread and milk; there *was* a frog in my bread and milk,' he repeated, with the insistence of a person skilled in argument who does not intend to move from an advantageous position.

So his boy-cousin and girl-cousin and his quite uninteresting younger brother were to be taken to the seaside at Jagborough that afternoon and he was to stay at home. His cousins' aunt, who insisted, by an unreasonable leap of the imagination, in calling herself his aunt also, had hurriedly invented the Jagborough trip in order to impress on Nicholas the delights that he had rightly lost by his bad behaviour at the breakfast-table. It was her habit, whenever one of the children misbehaved, to invent something enjoyable from which the offender would be banned. If all the children misbehaved collectively, they were suddenly informed of a **circus** in a neighbouring town, a circus of unusual quality and any number of elephants, to which, but for their misdeeds, they would have been taken that same day.

A few tears were expected from Nicholas when the moment for the departure of the expedition arrived. As a matter of fact, all the crying was done by his girl-cousin, who banged her knee rather painfully against the side of the car as she was jumping in.

'How she roared!' said Nicholas happily, as the party drove off without any show of the high spirits that they should have felt.

'She'll soon get over it,' said the so-called aunt. 'It will be a splendid afternoon for running about over those beautiful sands. How they'll enjoy themselves!'

'Bobby won't enjoy himself much, and he won't be able to run about much either,' said Nicholas with a bitter laugh. 'His boots are hurting him. They're too tight.'

'Why didn't he tell me they were hurting?' asked the aunt sharply.

'He told you twice, but you weren't listening. You often don't listen when we tell you important things.'

'You are not to go into the gooseberry garden,' said the aunt, changing the subject.

'Why not?' demanded Nicholas.

'Because you're being punished,' said the aunt, with an air of superiority.

Nicholas did not accept her line of reasoning: he felt that it was quite possible to be punished and in a gooseberry garden at the same time. His face took on a noticeably stubborn look. It was clear to his aunt that he was determined to get into the gooseberry garden, 'only', as she remarked to herself, 'because I have told him he is not to'.

Now the gooseberry garden had two doors into it, and once a small person like Nicholas had slipped in there, he could completely disappear from view in the forest of plants and bushes. The aunt had many other things to do that afternoon, but she spent an hour or two on unnecessary gardening tasks among the flower beds, from where she could keep an eye on the two doors that led to the forbidden area. She was a woman of few ideas but immense powers of concentration.

Nicholas made one or two appearances in the front garden, crawling with exaggerated caution towards one or other of the doors, but he was never able for a moment to escape the aunt's watchful eye. As a matter of fact, he had no intention of trying to get into the gooseberry garden, but it was extremely convenient for him that his aunt should believe that he had. It was a belief that would force her to remain on guard duty for most of the afternoon.

Having thoroughly excited her suspicions, Nicholas slipped back into the house and quickly carried out a plan of action that had been growing for a long time in his mind. By standing on a chair in the library, one could

*By standing on a chair in the library, one could reach a large, flat, important-looking key.*

reach a large, flat, important-looking key. The key was as important as it looked. It was the instrument which kept the mysteries of the **lumber**-room safe from the eyes of those who were not allowed to enter it, and which opened the way only for aunts and similar privileged persons. Nicholas had not much experience of the art of fitting keys into keyholes and turning locks, but for the last few days he had practised with the key of the schoolroom door. He did not believe in trusting too much to luck and accident. The key turned stiffly in the lock, but it turned. The door opened and Nicholas was in an unknown land, compared with which the gooseberry garden was a very ordinary delight, a much less rewarding pleasure.

Often and often, Nicholas had pictured to himself what the lumber-room might be like, that world which was so carefully shut away from youthful eyes and about which no questions were ever asked. It was every bit as fascinating as he had expected. In the first place, it was large and dimly lit, the only source of light being one high window opening on to the forbidden garden. In the second place, it was a storehouse of unimagined treasure. The so-called aunt was one of those people who think that things get spoiled with use and who put them away in dust and dampness as a way of keeping them safe. Those parts of the house which Nicholas knew best were rather bare and gloomy, but here there were wonderful things for the eye to enjoy.

First of all, there was a sewn picture with a wooden border, which was clearly meant to be a fire-screen. To Nicholas the picture was a living, breathing story. He sat down on a bundle of Indian cloth, glowing in wonderful colours beneath a layer of dust, and studied all the details of the sewn picture. A man, dressed in the hunting-costume of some far-off age, had just shot a deer with an arrow. It could not have been a difficult shot because the deer was only one or two steps away from him. In the thick mass of bushes suggested by the picture, it would not have been too difficult to creep up on a feeding deer, and the two black-and-white dogs that were leaping forward to join in the chase had obviously been trained to keep back until the arrow had been shot. That part of the picture was simple, though interesting. But did the huntsman see what Nicholas saw: that four wolves were advancing in his direction through the wood? There might be more than four of them hidden behind the trees, and in any case would the man and his dogs be able to fight off four wolves if they made an attack? The man had only two arrows left and he might miss with one or both of them; all one knew about his skill in shooting was that he could hit a large deer at laughably short range. Nicholas sat for many golden minutes considering the possibilities of the scene. He preferred to think that there were more than four wolves and that the man and his dogs were in a tight corner.

But there were other objects of delight and interest claiming his attention: here were strange twisted candle-holders in the form of snakes, and a teapot in the shape of a duck, out of whose mouth the tea was supposed to come. How dull and shapeless the teapot downstairs seemed in comparison! And there was an old wooden box packed with sweet-smelling cotton wool, and between the layers of cotton wool were little metal figures: horses and birds and devils, delightful to see and to handle. Less promising in appearance was a large square book with plain black covers. Nicholas opened it carefully and – how wonderful! – it was full of coloured pictures of birds. And such birds! In the garden and in the country roads when he went for a walk, Nicholas saw a few birds, though none of them was very big. Here were birds of enormous size, of every shape and colour, such as he had never dreamed of.

As he was admiring the colours of a Chinese duck and

imagining its life history, the voice of his aunt shouting his name came from the gooseberry garden outside. She had grown suspicious at his long disappearance and had immediately thought that he had climbed over the wall behind a screen of lilac trees. She was now carrying out an energetic and rather hopeless search for him among the fruit bushes and taller vegetables.

'Nicholas! Nicholas!' she screamed. 'You are to come out at once. It's no use trying to hide there; I can see you all the time.'

It was probably the first time for twenty years that someone had smiled in that lumber-room.

Soon the angry repetitions of Nicholas's name were replaced by a loud scream and a cry for somebody to come quickly. Nicholas shut the book, put it back carefully in its place in a corner and shook some dust from a neighbouring pile of newspapers over it. Then he crept from the room, locked the door and replaced the key exactly where he had found it. His aunt was still calling his name when he walked unhurriedly into the front garden.

'Who's calling?' he asked.

'Me,' came the answer from the other side of the wall. 'Didn't you hear me? I've been looking for you in the gooseberry garden, and I've fallen into the rain-water tank. Luckily there's no water in it, but the sides are slippery and I can't get out. Fetch the little ladder from under the apple tree –'

'I was told I wasn't to go into the gooseberry garden,' said Nicholas quickly.

'I told you not to and now I tell you that you may,' came the voice from the rain-water tank, rather impatiently.

'Your voice doesn't sound like aunt's,' objected Nicholas. 'You may be the Devil tempting me to be disobedient. Aunt often tells me that the Devil tempts me and that

I always give in. This time I'm not going to give in.'

'Don't talk nonsense,' said the prisoner in the tank. 'Go and fetch the ladder.'

'Will there be gooseberry jam for tea?' asked Nicholas innocently.

'Certainly there will be,' said the aunt, privately deciding that Nicholas should have none of it.

'Now I know that you are the Devil and not aunt,' shouted Nicholas joyfully. 'When we asked aunt for gooseberry jam yesterday, she said there wasn't any. I know there are four jars of it in the store-cupboard because I looked, and of course *you* know it's there, but *she* doesn't, because she said there wasn't any. Oh, Devil, you *have* given the game away!'

There was an unusual sense of luxury in being able to talk to an aunt as though one was talking to the Devil, but Nicholas knew with the sharp instinct of a child that such luxuries were not to be enjoyed for too long. He walked noisily away, and it was a kitchen-maid, in search of a lettuce, who finally rescued the aunt from the rain-water tank.

Tea that evening was eaten in gloomy silence. The tide had been at its highest when the children had arrived at Jagborough Beach, so there had been no sands to play on – a fact that the aunt had failed to consider in her hasty organization of the expedition. The tightness of Bobby's boots had had a disastrous effect on his temper the whole afternoon, and altogether it could not be said that the children had enjoyed themselves. The aunt maintained the frozen silence of someone who has suffered undeserved imprisonment in a rain-water tank for thirty-five minutes. As for Nicholas, he too was silent, with the silence of one who has much to think about. It was just possible, he considered, that the hunter and his dogs might escape, while the wolves were feeding on the body of the dying deer.

# EXERCISES

## Vocabulary Work

Look back at the 'Dictionary Words' in this book.
1 Find: a *five* words for ANIMALS
         b *three* words for FLOWERS or FRUIT
         c *three* words for LANGUAGE or WRITING
         d *two* words for MONEY
         e *two* words for HUMANS
2 Write short sentences to show the meaning of these words:
   *bush*, *bog*, *lining* (noun), *lumber*, *circus*, *masculine*, *scandal*.

## Comprehension

*Pages 1–30*
1 Name each of these people and say in which of the first four
  stories they appear.
  a A nervous visitor who thinks he has seen several ghosts.
  b A lady who has difficulty doing her hair.
  c A wanderer who is given shelter because he looks like some-
    one else.
  d A young lady who receives an unwanted umbrella for her
    birthday.

*Pages 31–54*
2 Answer these questions.
  a How did Louisa Mebbin benefit from the death of a tiger?
  b What *two* things did Ulrich von Gradwitz offer Georg Znaeym
    when they were both trapped under the fallen tree?
  c How did Matilda get Tarquin to go back to the pig-house?

*86*

d James Cushat-Prinkly is about to be disappointed by his new bride at the end of this story. Why?

*Pages 55–85*

3 Are the following sentences true (✓) or false (x)?

a Mrs Peter Pigeoncote is worried that Thieving Wilfred will steal one of her golden wedding presents.

b The young man who met Gortsby could not stay at the Patagonian Hotel because it had burned down in a fire.

c According to Tobermory, the only reason Lady Blemley invited Mavis Pellinton to her house party was because she hoped Mavis would be stupid enought to buy her old car.

d Nicholas found the key to the lumber room in the library.

4 What are the names of these people and in which story do they appear?

a A young man whose family want him to get married.

b A historian who writes the words for popular songs.

c A young woman who enjoys telling untrue stories.

d A house guest who is mistakenly thought to be a thief.

e A gentleman sitting in a London park who finds a cake of soap.

5 Animals appear in many of Saki's stories. In between three and five sentences, explain the following.

a How and why Mrs Packletide's tiger really died.

b How a cat alarmed Lady Blemley's house guests.

c How a large pig upset Mrs Stossen's social ambitions.

d How Nicholas, although he was being punished, found satisfaction in a picture of a deer and some wolves.

e How a silver fox damaged the friendship between two young women.

f How two badly injured men finally realized that their rescuers were dangerous animals.

## Discussion

1 Which of the people in these stories do you dislike most? Give reasons for your choice.
2 Many of these stories end in a way that the main person in the story doesn't expect. Choose one or two stories and compare what this person expected to happen with what *did* happen. Is the ending a reward or punishment?

## Writing

1 Look at the picture on page 59. Describe Peter Pigeoncote's appearance and what he is doing (150 words).
2 You are a newspaper reporter. Write a report (200 words) about Tobermory, the amazing talking cat!

## Review

Write a short review of this book (100 words) and say which story you liked the best, and why, and which story you liked the least, and why.